T0368415

LIVING
TO
THRIVE

a holistic guide to living with cancer

Kathryn White

BALBOA.PRESS

A DIVISION OF HAY HOUSE

Balboa Press books may be ordered through booksellers or by contacting:

Balboa Press
A Division of Hay House
1663 Liberty Drive
Bloomington, IN 47403
www.balboapress.com
844-682-1282

Because of the dynamic nature of the Internet, any web addresses or
links contained in this book may have changed since publication and
may no longer be valid. The views expressed in this work are solely those
of the author and do not necessarily reflect the views of the publisher,
and the publisher hereby disclaims any responsibility for them.

The author of this book does not dispense medical advice or prescribe the use
of any technique as a form of treatment for physical, emotional, or medical
problems without the advice of a physician, either directly or indirectly. The
intent of the author is only to offer information of a general nature to help
you in your quest for emotional and spiritual well-being. In the event you use
any of the information in this book for yourself, which is your constitutional
right, the author and the publisher assume no responsibility for your actions.

Print information available on the last page.

ISBN: 979-8-7652-5656-5 (sc)
ISBN: 979-8-7652-5655-8 (e)

Library of Congress Control Number: 2024921855

Balboa Press rev. date: 10/30/2024

For Jonathan, Jackson, and Joshua.

You are the three greatest loves of my life,

my rocks, and my reason.

Contents

Contents

Foreword

In a world that often emphasizes survival, Kathryn White's *Living to Thrive: a holistic guide to living with cancer*, stands as a beacon of hope and empowerment for those navigating the complexities of a cancer diagnosis. This book is not just a recounting of a journey but a comprehensive guide to transforming the experience of living with cancer into an opportunity for growth, healing, and thriving.

Kathryn, a self-described cancer Thriver, invites readers to look beyond the initial shock of diagnosis and to embrace a holistic approach that nurtures not only the body but also the mind and spirit. Her message is clear: while we may not choose the challenges we face, we can choose how we respond to them. This guide is a testament to the resilience of the human spirit and the power of a positive mindset.

Living to Thrive: a holistic guide to living with cancer, is filled with practical advice, personal anecdotes and empowering strategies. Kathryn shares her wisdom on topics ranging from nutrition and physical activity to emotional resilience and self-love. She encourages readers to listen to their inner voice, reject limiting prognoses, and embrace a mindset that sees beyond survival to a thriving, fulfilling life.

This book is an invitation to reclaim your life and redefine what it means to live with cancer. Kathryn's compassionate and candid voice provides a comforting and inspiring companion for anyone facing this challenge. Whether you are a patient, a caregiver, or a loved one, *Living to Thrive: a holistic guide to living with cancer*, offers valuable insights and tools to help you navigate this path with grace and strength.

May this book serve as a guide and a source of comfort, inspiring you to take control of your narrative and live fully, courageously and with an open heart. As Kathryn beautifully illustrates, thriving is not just possible; it is within reach for all of us.

Carl Wagner
CEO
Center for Advancement in Cancer Education
www.beatcancer.org

My Fellow Thriver...

My name is Kathryn and I am a cancer Thriver. For a few years now, people have been telling me that I should write this book to share the story of my stage 4 colon cancer diagnosis and the work I have done so that I could inspire others to also thrive.

What I have learned, is that while caught up in trying not to die, I was actually learning how to live and put myself on a path to do more than just survive. Although full of fear and lacking in knowledge, I was committed to living, but did not have the tools to proceed. I had to re-educate myself and create a way to live that felt better physically, emotionally, and spiritually.

On December 22, 2015 I walked out of the chemotherapy suite and ceremoniously rang the bell. That day was the beginning of a new me and a new way of living. That was when I was ready to start doing the work to reclaim my life and transform my health.

My hope for you is that you can also feel ready to reclaim your life and learn that there is another way to live with cancer. My invitation to you is to trust yourself, get curious about what is available to you, and believe that you can do this.

This book is not a story, rather it is a guide to help you on your way towards being a thriver. Some of the information will resonate with you. There will be moments of great revelation that will help you find the pieces of the puzzle that are missing. Some of the information may feel overwhelming and you may not be ready for it yet. I didn't make all the changes at once. My work has been a process of actively seeking information and stumbling across wisdom. It has been a process of trying things when others thought I was a bit crazy and then deciding if what I had discovered was going to become part of my life.

Learning how to thrive is a process of reinventing yourself, seeking and gathering tools, and breaking old bad habits to create space for new good ones. I encourage you to become curious, to embrace change, to enjoy the process, and to lean into all the possibilities that are available to you. Settle into a sense of ease knowing that you are taking steps to love and support yourself.

Here is what is available to you in the coming chapters:

Chapter 1 - *The Club You Never Want to Join.* This chapter delves into how life can change in an instant. I talk about the overwhelming and surreal reality of having cancer when you never imagined yourself being there. I explore the questions that arise after diagnosis and choices you have in your cancer story.

Chapter 2 - *You Are Not Your Diagnosis.* This is where we uncover the difference between *having* a diagnosis and *being* your diagnosis. This is where you start to accept that cancer is now part of your life, and how this concept can make a difference moving forward. This chapter ends by talking about your prognosis and the power and impact of hearing the statistics.

Chapter 3 - *Vulnerability*. This is the beginning of the emotional work. I discuss how to be vulnerable so that you can ask for help. I explore the common statement that people just don't get it and then talk about how to use your new superpower to get the support you need and want.

Chapter 4 - *Live in the Present*. Living in the present is important when navigating cancer. In this chapter, I talk about being careful not to dwell in the past or get lost in the future. Here, we explore doing inner work that includes letting go of what was, so that you can step into what is and will be, and look at the things that have held you back or that are creating anxiety about the future. This inner work can support your outer work of doing and being a thriver.

Chapter 5 - *The Family*. Cancer impacts everyone in your family and it can be difficult to navigate. In this chapter, I share a few personal perspectives from my family and share thoughts on how to support your children, the impact on the caregiver, healing as a family, and the unexpected gift that can result.

Chapter 6 - *The Scars We Carry.* This chapter explores the physical and emotional scars that are now part of you. The scars on your body may physically impact your life. Then there are those emotional scars and triggers as a result of your traumatic experience.

Chapter 7 – *Things That Set You Off.* As you navigate cancer there will be moments that are emotionally challenging. From what is happening around you, to people who tell you their cancer stories, to ongoing tests, there are a lot of emotions to manage. Here I share a strategy I created that helps you support yourself when it feels like things are getting out of control.

Chapter 8 - *Rebuild Your Foundation.* Nutrition and movement build the foundation of your body to assist in carrying you through and beyond the cancer process. Here I share how you can support your body through lifestyle changes that can make a big difference.

Chapter 9 - *You're Stronger Than You Think.* Your thoughts are powerful and so are your words. This chapter explores the traditional fight language around cancer, offering a different way to talk to yourself about what is happening in your life. I delve into the body's stress response in order to move you out of fight or flight and start moving towards thriving in life.

Chapter 10 - *Believe in Yourself.* This chapter is all about you, the real person living with cancer. I share with you the empowerment of self-love and self-belief, and how these two things are so important to help you move through the diagnosis, into treatment, and then to rebuilding your post-cancer life.

Chapter 11 - *Living to Thrive.* In this final chapter I share the inspirational phone call that changed everything for me and that will help you to get on the path to being a thriver.

There are some principles to follow to help you get started. You will start to notice a subtle shift in yourself and gain some powerful wisdom and knowledge that you can bring into your life. You will start to hear a voice within you reminding you that you have choices on this path to thriving. This is where self-belief grows, where you see what is available to you, and why self-belief is a key part in choosing your own path. You can accept what feels right for you and put aside what doesn't serve you right now. It will still be there when you are ready.

As you move through this work, you will notice that you feel lighter, that the weight of the diagnosis is lifting from your shoulders, and creating a space inside of you that allows you to breathe more freely. You will find yourself more connected to your heart and more in tune with your emotional self, a side of you that you may have never known or that you left behind somewhere along the way in your life. Here is where you start to feel and honour your emotions while allowing them to move through you rather than pushing them down.

Cancer can take away self-belief and replace it with blame and shame. It can create fear and doubt. I am going to show you tools that you can integrate into your healing process.

I will share with you the idea of loving yourself. Self-love will help you to heal. Loving yourself so much that you are willing to take action to move from survivor to thriver is the best gift you can give yourself. Learning to love yourself will help you to release old narratives and embrace new stories that you get to create. This is a key part of the path that leaves the old survivor mindset behind and guides you towards thriving.

You can do this.
Together we can do this - let me be your guide.
Kathryn

My Philosophy

You can do difficult things by believing
in yourself and possibility.

There is life with cancer.

Every day is 100%.

Say yes to fun.

Mindset matters.

Thoughts are just stories you tell yourself.

There is life outside of the doctor's office.

Living with cancer is a body, mind,
and spirit experience.

Life is meant to be lived in the present.

Learning to thrive is the best work you will ever do.

Chapter 1

The Club You Never Wanted to Join

but here you are

My Oncologist: You have stage 4 colon cancer.
Me: Blank stare, blank mind, barely able to hear,
mostly unable to process words.

Life is full of surprises and doesn't always turn out the way you imagined. The road of life is full of twists and turns and the choices you make shape you along the way. Every decision, even the small ones, lay the foundation of your future. The interesting part is that the results of your choices might not show up immediately. Sometimes, it takes a while for them to reveal themselves – perhaps when you least expect it. What happens next is up to you.

How do you navigate the unexpected? What do you do when everything changes in an instant and you find yourself in a new place?

Life Can Change In An Instant

In January 2015 I was on a six month sabbatical from my teaching job. My husband and I had big plans to travel and enjoy my time away from work. Lingering in the background were signs that something was wrong with my body – feeling tired all the time, struggling to catch my breath, aching on one side, and noticeable changes in my digestive system. We had been questioning these symptoms for months but kept coming up against a brick wall. My doctor was not concerned about what was happening. Even after an ultrasound showed spots on my liver, he brushed off the results as a red herring, refusing to talk about cancer even when we told him we were worried. I reminded him that my father had died of stage 4 colon cancer when I was 22 years old but he continued to investigate other medical conditions and not to pursue cancer as a real possibility. He decided I had a gastric bleed and was treating me for that diagnosis.

My doctor sent me for an MRI and an upper GI scope. When I started to talk to the surgeon about the symptoms I was experiencing, he listened and decided to switch the procedure to a colonoscopy instead. My surgeon couldn't complete the colonoscopy because I actually had a blockage in my colon, not an upper GI problem. That surgeon's decision to listen to me saved my life. I was terrified but I was also grateful that he had listened to me and that he was moving forward with further tests and surgery.

In preparation for the colon blockage surgery I met with my family doctor for the routine pre-surgery checkup of weight, height, and blood pressure. Because I didn't think it was going to be anything more than a check-up, I went in by myself. When my doctor came into the room, he delivered the results of my MRI which indicated that they were 99% sure that I had cancer. I was so angry. I couldn't understand how he could have known what he was going to tell me and not suggest to have my husband with me for support, especially after we had expressed our concerns about cancer with him. The rush of anger and disbelief was incredibly powerful. My whole world changed in an instant.

The shock hit me once more when my oncologist confirmed the diagnosis of stage 4 colon cancer. Everything froze in that moment. I felt the colour drain from my face and I couldn't quite grasp the weight of what I was being told. I turned to my husband, looking to him for answers. I wanted to say something, to understand what was happening, but my mind was cloudy. Words and thoughts slipped away from me while the oncologist's words sunk in. I had witnessed this before. I knew the face of stage 4 colon cancer. Two decades ago, I stood by my father when this very diagnosis claimed his life.

The Club You Never Wanted To Join

Since my earliest memories as a child participating in team sports and clubs, I felt that they were more than just activities. They were places where I found friends who shared my interests and where I belonged. As I grew up, my involvement expanded into professional teams as a teacher. This reinforced how crucial community was for me. These groups weren't just about fitting in; they became platforms for me to grow personally, collaborate, and find support.

Being told I had cancer changed everything in an instant. Suddenly, I was part of a club I never knew about nor wanted to join. It's a club that issues you a membership you never asked for and there's no giving it back. Joining appears to come with no perks or advantages. Being a member of this club means you've been told you have cancer, but it goes beyond that.

The cancer clubhouse is not a happy place. It is a sombre spot where members sit in the clinic, waiting for their names or numbers to be called for appointments or treatments. Everyone is there for the same reason, some are putting on a brave face, but wishing they were anywhere else in that moment.

In my years as a certified holistic cancer coach, I've heard the struggles of my clients as they try to understand why this has happened to them. Many seek to find a source, something to blame, a moment or action to direct their pain and anger towards. They want to know the why and how, searching for the moment they believe led to their cancer diagnosis. It's a natural reaction to want to find a source of blame. This provides a focus, a way to avoid dealing with overwhelming emotions of vulnerability, loneliness, and most of all fear.

There is a flip side to being a club member, however, in a community that brings hope and possibilities you may never have considered. I see this in my cancer coaching clients as they show up for themselves and do the work to reclaim their lives and transform their health as they move from survivor to thriver. Each conversation is a source of inspiration both for them and for me, that directly allows each of us to learn and grow separately and yet together. While everyone's experience is unique, we all have common thoughts, fears, and hopes.

Navigating this club can lead to discovering a new and improved version of yourself you never knew could exist. It provides the opportunity to challenge your preconceived notions about cancer, rethink your language surrounding your diagnosis, and change your mindset. It's about stepping up and facing the challenges and digging deeper into your resolve than you ever thought possible. From within, you find hope and strength. It's an opportunity for self-discovery and personal growth, a chance to hit the reset button on your life, and to become a new version of yourself like a phoenix rising from the ashes. When you choose to dive in and work hard you inevitably learn more about yourself and grow as a person.

This membership brings physical and emotional challenges, but it also opens up infinite possibilities and opportunities, which together we will explore in the upcoming chapters. In yoga teachings, they say where there's darkness, there's also light.

You Have Choices

You get the diagnosis and have a plan for treatment, so what comes next? This is where many people feel stuck. Being diagnosed is a surreal moment where life goes from normal to suddenly feeling out of control. It's a place you never thought would be your reality, yet here you are, facing an unexpected turn in your life's story, standing at a crossroads with a map that has two paths. The first path leads you to passively accept the situation, while the second path is where you choose to take action and reclaim control of your life. You have to make a choice between one of two very different mindsets, the inaction of the powerless patient, or the action of the engaged thriver.

My path became clear with one message. Shortly after my colon surgery, I was home recovering and found myself in bed for most of the day. One day in particular I recall telling myself, "I can't do this. This is hard. I don't want to do this." In that moment I had decided to pull the covers over my head and quit on myself. Inaction and powerless was to be my path.

Before pulling the covers over my head I opened my messages to find one in particular that caught my eye. A guy I went to school with, and whom I had not seen in over 20 years was at the top of my messages. I decided to read it, curious as to what he may have to say. What his message read was this, *"I just wanted you to know that I am thinking about you today."* Short, simple, and life changing. In that moment I decided that if this friend from my past could take two minutes out of his life to send me a note of kindness, then I needed to get over myself and out of my own way.

In that moment I decided to live, to take action, and to do everything I had to in order to survive. I promised myself that I would get up every day, put on my big girl pants, and move forward one day at a time. I chose my path. What's yours? Can you be open to receiving a sign and an opportunity to choose the second path of engaged survivor? Perhaps it's a message from a friend, an inspirational post on social media, or maybe it is reading this book.

I choose to take charge and be an empowered thriver. If I have to be in this unwanted club, I want to do it my way. What I am sure about is that I won't let others tell me how to live. I get to control my choices. Throughout the sections of this book, you will see the many opportunities for you to choose your path to thriving.

Moving Forward

I avoid using the term "journey" when talking about my experience with cancer and I've noticed many of my coaching clients feel the same way. The word has become so common that it almost feels cliche. Some clients feel like it puts them onto a path they can't control. Personally, when I hear "journey", it feels like there's a final destination and I'm just along for the ride.

Instead, I like to say it's my walk with cancer. This brings me a sense of calm and control. It makes me feel like I can slow down and really take in what's happening. This perspective supports the important steps of accepting the diagnosis and taking action. Even though dealing with cancer involves a lot of self-reflection and discovery which could happen on a journey, I find the idea of walking with it more in line with how I approach things. You can call it whatever feels right for you, but for me, journey won't be a part of the conversation. Part of this process is about finding language that fits with how you see and handle things. So, whether it's a walk, a path, or something else, the important thing is feeling in control and at peace with your own experience.

We may have similarities and differences in how we are navigating this new version of ourselves because everyone has a unique story. My desire is to share the strategies and insights I've discovered and to give you the information you need to make choices about what's available to you and to create change in your life. Even small changes can make a big difference. Remember, you have the power to shape your story.

Thriver Lessons:

∗ Never go to an appointment alone.

∗ You have choices.

∗ Everyone's cancer story will be different.

Episodes from the

"Living to Thrive with Cancer" Podcast

In the *"Living to Thrive with Cancer"* Podcast listeners are reminded that life with cancer can be embraced from a place of self-love and self-advocacy. Tune in as I share uplifting and insightful episodes on navigating life with a positive perspective.

Let's Get Started

Learn who I am and why I'm here – let's kickstart your life of living to thrive with cancer.

Sharing Your Diagnosis

When it comes to a cancer diagnosis, sharing your news can be a no brainer or it can be a really big decision. Here we unravel the ins and outs of who to tell, what to tell, and when to tell.

When You Are Just Pissed Off

Learn more about why it's okay to feel angry, but also why you want to learn how to manage that anger so it doesn't control your life.

Being Part of the Process

You get to be in control of the parts of your life that you can control, how you view yourself, and how you see yourself in the process.

5 Lessons from a Cancer Thriver

Learn the five discoveries that helped me to navigate life with cancer.

"Healing takes courage, and we all have courage, even if we have to dig a little to find it."

– Tori Amos

Chapter 2

You Are Not Your Diagnosis

accept the diagnosis;
reject the prognosis

Me to my husband: I don't want to be known as Kathryn the cancer patient. I don't want to be a label.

It takes some time to internalize the shocking news and the reality that you have cancer. There is a lot of fear around death, the chances of survival, and worry around your family. Perhaps you are still processing all of this, or perhaps you are moving through the cancer treatment process. You may even be living post-treatment, trying to reclaim your life and figure out how to move forward. To help you do that, I want to share with you one of the most important and powerful thoughts that you can tell yourself: You are not your diagnosis.

You Are Not Your Diagnosis

One of the first thoughts I share with my clients is that you are not your diagnosis. There is a difference between having a diagnosis and being your diagnosis. I remember one of the first things I said to my husband was that I didn't want to be known as 'Kathryn, the cancer patient.' From the beginning, I knew this was my new reality, but I was not going to let it be my identity.

It is important to separate you the person in this situation from the medical diagnosis which is happening in your body. This is the beginning of changing your mindset and the beginning of deciding that it is not my cancer, it is the cancer. This subtle shift from my to the makes all the difference. You do not own the cancer; it is not your identity.

The Power of Acceptance

One of the biggest shifts you can make is to accept, although it may be difficult at first, that you have cancer and that this is happening in your life.

As a yoga teacher I have learned that when your thoughts and actions are aligned towards positivity and hope, you are more inclined to release a "victim" mentality and embrace an "empowered" mentality. This is the first step on your path to thriving. In yoga teachings, they say where there's darkness, there's also light.

The Power of Rejection

You can choose to reject the prognosis that is assigned to your condition. I rejected any idea that numbers were going to dictate my life. Instead, I chose to live in the belief of a 100% chance of surviving. Other people feel the need to know. That is your choice.

To this day, I do not know my prognosis. Not knowing allows me to feel empowered and to believe in possibility. I believe that this is a key factor in my story.

If your doctor gives you the statistics about your type and stage of cancer, they do not have to be your reality, rather consider them as other peoples' numbers. This data is based on research gathered from other people based on a specific cancer. They include people of all ages and health conditions who have been diagnosed with the same type of cancer. What is not considered is patient history.

Each person is an individual with their own life history, where they were raised, how they were raised, what they ate, the air they breathed, their exposure to toxins and their genetics. We can't measure these variables and they are not considered in the statistics. The potential problem with statistics is that they may create a limitation in your mind and around your hope. Living by these numbers can cause you to fixate on what may be rather than living right now. Don't live by the numbers and don't put limits on yourself. There is a lot of power in taking control of your life and in believing that you can do this.

Thriver Lessons:

* ✳ You are not your diagnosis.

* ✳ Statistics will mess with your mind.

* ✳ Other peoples' numbers aren't yours.

Episodes from the

"Living to Thrive with Cancer" Podcast

You Are Not Your Diagnosis

We do not need to accept our cancer diagnosis as our new identity. There is life with cancer and you do not have to be your diagnosis.

Be An Exceptional Cancer Thriver

There are unique qualities that support cancer patients in rising above their prognosis to create a thriving life with cancer. Explore what exceptional means and why this is important information to know if you are living with cancer.

Acceptance and Rejection

Accepting your diagnosis is the first step in moving forward with cancer. The second step is related to your prognosis. Do you have to accept and be the statistics around your diagnosis? There is another way, a way that can help you to thrive with cancer.

> *"Acceptance opens the door for growth and transformation."*
>
> *- Eckhart Tolle*

Chapter 3

Vulnerability

your superpower

---

*Friends and family: Just let us know what you need or
if we can do anything to help you.
Me: How do I know what to ask for when
I have never done this before?*

A cancer diagnosis can be a rallying cry. It calls in
people that you know and even people that you don't
know who want to be supportive. People truly want
to help and will make the offer to do whatever you
need. Some will show up with gifts, flowers, and food.
Others will send notes or messages of support. This
is great. Support is exactly what is needed when your
life has been turned upside down and even the littlest
things feel like big tasks, but how do you know what
you need and, who and how many people do you want

to let into this very personal part of your life? It can be difficult to navigate support and other peoples' desire to help when you are processing and moving through what has happened and trying to figure out what your next steps are.

Being Vulnerable

One of the most difficult things for me in my life has been giving myself permission to ask for help. Growing up, I developed a very strong sense of independence and this façade that I could do everything myself. In my mind, not being independent was a weakness and so instead over the years I decided to only count on myself because placing trust in others to be there when I needed them required vulnerability. Vulnerability was not something I was willing to embrace.

Consider vulnerability as two concepts: being vulnerable, and having ability. Inside of vulnerability lies ability. It is the ability to make choices and decisions around things you have never done or imagined yourself ever doing. The ability to harness the courage to admit you need support. The ability to take back some control in your life when you feel like it has all been taken away. You have to allow in complete strangers and trust them with your health and your life. You have to let others support you, provide for you, and lift you up when you are down. You have to trust and believe in yourself on a level you may never have experienced before. You can experience vulnerability and ability at the same time.

How to Be Vulnerable

Moving through the cancer process requires you to be vulnerable. You have to share more about yourself with strangers than you ever thought you would. You are literally baring yourself physically to tests, scans and poking and prodding by people you don't know or have a relationship with. You have to trust the most sacred thing you have to the experience of others – yourself – not just your physical self, but also your emotional self.

There are three things that I have identified that need to be considered when talking about being vulnerable. Knowing and understanding these parts will allow you to start feeling more confident when you decide to ask for help. There is no particular order, only the order that feels right for you.

> ✳ **Accept that this is happening in your life.** Realistically, you have to admit that there is a problem or situation that needs support in order to be able to ask for support. If you ignore or

deny what is happening, pretending that nothing is wrong, you are actually doing yourself a disservice on many levels. Acceptance doesn't mean you have to like what is happening; it just creates space for you to move forward. When it comes to asking for help, you have to know that there is a problem, acknowledge the problem, and get to a place where you know that you cannot and do not have to do this alone.

* **Give yourself permission to accept and receive.** Cancer is mysterious. A diagnosis lands you in a world that you may have heard about but have never seen other than through movies, TV, or the experiences of people you know. It is difficult to live in an unfamiliar world where there are so many unknowns. You have to be brave to move forward. This requires accepting that it is alright to not know what to do, and to ask the people who do know what to do for help. It requires you to be open and willing to receive.

* **Trust yourself and others.** Your health and wellness are so deeply personal that you may feel protective of them. People need to feel safe and have trust before they can ask for help. Sharing that there is something about yourself

that you believe to be less than ideal, requires you to admit that you want to make a change but don't know what to do, or where to start. That makes you vulnerable and open to judgement and criticism, perceived or real. It takes courage to look at yourself and say, "Now is the time. Now is when I need to do something."

Asking for Help is a Superpower

When you see yourself as being both vulnerable and having the ability to harness that vulnerability, you can get the support you need and deserve. This can be a pivotal moment in how you approach life with cancer. You don't have to do this alone. It takes courage to admit you need support. This is why asking for help is a superpower.

Using Your Superpower

* Decide that you are going to take some control. Knowing you have a superpower is a game changer. The first step is to decide that you are going to take some control and find your voice. Be willing to tell people what you need. This is not selfish. This is self-love. If you want something and other people have no idea, tell

them. It is likely they will do it, and that is a win for you. They just want you to be happy and healthy. You may wonder why you have to tell friends and family what you want and need. They should just do it, right? Wrong. Here is the thing… they don't get it. They don't understand what is happening to you and why you have certain needs. The truth is, you don't want them to get it. For someone to truly get it they must have lived a similar experience, meaning they have to have had cancer too. What you really want is for them to hear you and support you.

✶ **Be clear.** Next, you need to be clear. You may need to tell your loved ones what you need, and how you need them to support your choices and decisions. The loving friends and family in your life may not understand why you are taking certain actions in your life. What is important to remember is that how they react and respond is coming from a place of love and concern for you. They can't read your mind, or feel your thoughts, or put themselves in your shoes. They can only see you as you are now and make comparisons to who you were and how you behaved before cancer. Ask and receive from a place of love. Examples of support you can ask for can include carrying your laundry up and down for you, cutting your lawn, picking up kids from school and activities, getting groceries, picking up a book at the library, and preparing and dropping off healthy meals.

✳ **Decide that asking for support is not difficult**. Finally, you need to *decide that asking for support is not difficult*. You can create or even co-create the life you want in the present. Sitting down and having a conversation about your desires and needs, balanced with reality and the needs of your loved ones, is not unreasonable. Be open to sharing, but also be open to hearing. It may not feel easy at first, but the more you believe that you are worthy of receiving support and are able to be vulnerable, the easier it will be to reach out to voice your needs and wishes.

Invest In Yourself

Asking for help is a way of investing in yourself. It is you saying that you want to find a better way, a different way, or even just the way to help yourself. It is you emotionally investing in your health and happiness. This is the beginning of believing that it is safe and good to have others help you. It requires you to show up for yourself and to risk being vulnerable. Acknowledging who you are, what you need, and that you perhaps cannot do it alone, is the bravest and the best thing you can do for yourself.

Thriver Lessons:

* Vulnerability is a strength, not a weakness.

* Tell people what you need.

* Asking for help is a superpower.

Episodes from the

"Living to Thrive with Cancer" Podcast

When They Just Don't Get It

Cancer patients often experience a sense of isolation as others may struggle to understand their illness. A shift in perspective can foster better understanding and support.

From Teacher to Coach

In this episode I talk about becoming a coach and how I had to change my thoughts around my role to step into becoming a Cancer Coach.

Relationships that Support Your Healing

It takes support to move through a life-threatening illness like cancer. Support can make a difference in how you work through your life with cancer.

Protecting vs Sharing

While the instinct to protect loved ones is natural, withholding the cancer diagnosis may hinder personal healing. Being able to open up about your cancer diagnosis is part of the healing process.

Asking for Help is a Superpower

Embracing vulnerability and recognizing the strength in seeking help can create a powerful shift for the individual who once viewed it as a weakness.

"Ask for help. Not because you are weak. But because you want to remain strong."

– Les Brown

Chapter 4

Live in the Present

resisting the pull of the past and the future

My chemo team: You're all done.
Go out and live your life.
Me: How do I do that when I don't
even know who I am anymore?

Almost four years out from my original cancer diagnosis, I found a small lump in my abdomen near my original colon surgery scar. Needless to say, it sent me into a panic. Immediately my mind went to the worst case so I got myself to the doctor, went for a biopsy and sure enough, it was cancer.

My brain immediately relived all the scenarios of needing surgery, having to do chemotherapy again and feeling sick and tired all of the time. It wanted to keep me stuck in the negative thoughts and feelings that are meant to protect me but instead it set off emotions of overwhelming fear and stress. This setback was devastating because I was just starting to feel normal and healthy again and was moving forward in my life. When I shared this news with my family, they immediately reverted to survival mode; we were all angry and afraid because we had been here before. Inside of ourselves we were carrying all this raw unprocessed emotion from the past few years that none of us knew how to release in a healthy way.

What I knew was that we couldn't keep feeling like this. So, as a family we decided to take out our anger through a healthy and controlled activity.

As we explored our options for spending time together on one of our now regular Mandatory Family Fun Days, we discovered a nearby axe throwing venue. It seemed like the perfect activity for our family. Really it was win-win as we were able to spend time together as a family, we all got to throw things, and we were able to do a lot of yelling. We walked away from that night with a much needed emotional release that felt so good. It was a great way for us to collectively express our anger and grief.

That activity, even if it was just for that evening, helped us to resist the pull of reliving the past. It also kept us from projecting into an unknown future which we couldn't control. Instead, we were aware of our emotions and vented through throwing and yelling as we moved those emotions through our bodies. For just a few hours, we got to be a normal family again not the family facing another cancer recurrence. In that moment we were living in the present.

The Call of the Past

It is part of the human experience to hold onto and replay in our minds things that have harmed us. Stress, fear, trauma, regret, anger and sadness are all negative emotions that elicit an instinctive reaction within us that the brain responds to. It does this as a primitive survival mechanism known as fight or flight. When you replay scenarios and emotions in your mind, your brain perceives it as a threat and responds by flooding you with the stress hormone cortisol, slowing down unnecessary bodily functions, and hindering your logical thinking and reasoning. In response to your emotions, the brain reverts to protecting you by preparing your body to escape the perceived threat that it thinks is happening.

In this way, as I like to say, your brain is a jerk. It wants to be helpful but, unmanaged, it may hold you back and keep you in fight or flight. This is an unhealthy loop to live in because of the impact on your body and your mind. This can be a consequence of holding onto the past.

One significant conversation that often comes up with clients in my coaching practice is around their thoughts and fears that their lifestyle choices are at the root cause of their diagnosis. In essence, they feel that they have done this to themselves. In response to this I ask them if they really need or want to know why they got cancer. How will this help them move forward in their life? Will knowing the answers to these questions be in their best interest since they can't change the cancer diagnosis? These are helpful questions to reflect on when trying to get out of living in the past.

You cannot change the past, but what you can change is how you think and what you choose to reflect on. Believing that you did not do this to yourself is very important. Instead, it is supportive of your emotional well-being to shift the thought towards what you are going to do to bring change into your life. This shifts you forward into the present and allows you to start taking control of your thoughts, actions, and goals.

After my recurrence when I started to realise that I was stuck in my old thoughts, I knew that I needed a new approach to living with cancer. To get the support I needed, I started to work with a life coach. She helped me to be mindful of my thoughts and to start dealing with the difficult emotions that I had pushed down and ignored. As I started to become aware of what I was thinking, I was able to start identifying what thoughts and emotions I was holding on to. This allowed me to process what I was feeling, let go of self-limiting thoughts, and start seeing a future that included knowing how to navigate my life with cancer.

Changing my thoughts has allowed me to forgive myself, and release my guilt for the cancer diagnosis as well as the impact it has had on my family. I have been able to reframe my thoughts about how my life has changed in a good way. This has made all the difference in my ability to create healthy habits that include eating healthier, practising mindfulness and gratitude in my life, thinking supportive thoughts, and seeing my life with cancer in a more positive and hopeful way.

Mark Twain said that, "Anger is an acid that can do more harm to the vessel in which it is stored than to anything on which it is poured." Holding on to emotions, burying them, and leaving them unprocessed is not just unhealthy for your emotional well-being, it is also unhealthy for your physical body. Angry thoughts create a disconnect in the messages you send to your brain and your body around wanting to get better. Anger also increases the stress response in your body which increases inflammation, creates tension in your muscles, and creates thoughts that are fear filled and angry. Your body heals better when it is in a state of calm and rest, and when you release the unease brought about by unresolved anger.

The Fear of the Future

When I was going through treatment, thinking about and planning for the future was really difficult for me. I struggled with thoughts around whether or not I would even be part of the future and what that would look like for my family. I cried when I was asked to make short term decisions because I felt like I was living day to day and was overwhelmed by what lay ahead of me. Cancer had such a strong grip on me that I couldn't even see beyond the next treatment, never mind envisioning future plans for a life after cancer when every effort in that moment was about day-to-day survival.

Transitioning into the post treatment phase is a time of mixed emotions. There are a lot of positive things to look forward to once treatment is done. You and the people around you will be excited that you have rung the bell signifying the completion of treatment and that you can now celebrate the end of this part of your cancer story. This is a big moment. You have done the work, endured the process, and now you have been told to go back to living your life. The question is, what does that mean and what does that look like? How do you just pick up from where you left off before your diagnosis and go back to the way things were when everything about cancer has changed you?

There can be so much relief in being done treatment, but with it can come a profound sense of insecurity when the time between medical visits gets longer. I know my anxiety increased when the frequency and time between my doctor appointments went from every two weeks to every three months. Ironically, I was stuck in a loop of needing the doctor's reassurance that there was no evidence of disease through regular visits, even though I was wishing I didn't have to go to any appointments at all. My doctor was my security blanket as I tried to move forward in my life.

Moving forward can be an emotional roller coaster. You may be celebrating yourself and the successful completion of treatment in one moment, while in the next you are wondering how this happened and what you do next. Then there is the thought of what if it comes back? It is important to acknowledge that this is a very difficult, very real, and very normal thought. Every ache and pain, every twinge, every cough can send you into an emotional spiral. It is a type of panic that is impossible to put into words, and for the people you love to understand.

Living in the Present

The greatest gift you can give yourself is learning how to be present. It is so liberating to live life right now rather than lamenting the past or fearing the future. Staying in the present means not sitting in uncertainty, which inevitably drags you back to negative emotions concerning the past and future. When you can see how awesome your life can be in the present, you can start to make plans and get excited about living and doing things that bring you joy.

This of course is going to look different for each of you because cancer is unique to everyone. The challenge that cancer patients face is that there is no one prescribed plan that fits every person. As you keep moving forward, you must discover what feels right in your life and start doing it. Mindset and mindfulness practices can support living in the present, which helps you avoid projecting into negative or fearful thoughts or situations that may never happen in the future. This is a key part of learning how to live with cancer.

How to Stay Present

* **Keep A Journal.** This practice is not about making mundane detailed entries of your daily activities. This practice is about noticing and recording your thoughts and feelings when they come up. Ask yourself the following questions: What are you thinking right now? Where is that thought showing up as a feeling in your body? (ex. tightness in your stomach, tension in your jaw, headaches), and how would acknowledging that thought and managing it help you to resolve that thought right now? Another journaling exercise is to use the thought reflection process of, "I feel...", "Because..." "But instead I choose..." Using a journal to record your thoughts will help you to see patterns and to identify what is setting you off and therefore help you to find solutions and resolution.

* **Start A Gratitude Practice.** Being grateful for what you have and for the good things in your

life helps to rewire your thoughts and elevate your emotions positively. You can write down what you are thankful for in a journal, keep a gratitude jar where you store little papers with your thoughts on them, or even just say what you are thankful for out loud. Writing and saying what you are grateful for can help you to internalize it, which in turn can help you to be in the present.

* **Practise Letting Go.** Every day, think of things or situations that you want to release from your consciousness. These may be people or situations, past or present, that have wounded you – let that situation go. Release judgments of yourself or others. Letting go of the things that are outside of your control will bring in ease and will help you to feel emotionally, and perhaps even physically, lighter.

* **Create A Mindfulness Practice.** This can be meditation, yoga, forest bathing, grounding, or some form of art. Anything that moves your attention to inside of yourself rather than outside of yourself creates mindfulness.

✳ **Accept Your Current Situation.** When you can accept that cancer is happening in your life, you can start to move forward and be present for yourself as you become more self-aware.

✳ **Find Balance in Control.** Cancer can make you feel like you have lost all control in your life. The truth is that you haven't. There are a lot of things that you can control which can bring you joy, but to find them you also need to let go of things that are beyond your control. Start with easier things like taking care of your well-being and choosing to do things that bring you joy. Little victories will help you to see that you do have some control in your life.

✳ **Learn to Move Through Difficult Emotions.** To live in the present, you must first learn to see and feel your difficult emotions such as grief, anger, or shame. It's not easy but acknowledging these emotions and understanding where they are coming from can turn things around for you and create space for positive emotions and joy to come into your life.

* **Learn How to Calm Yourself.** Stress and overwhelm may feel like a regular part of your life but they don't have to control it. You can learn skills and techniques to calm yourself when you need to. By doing so, you help your brain adapt to more positive connections that allow you to create space for joy. Learn more about mindfulness and meditation to help you to slow down and focus on the moment. Learn how to connect to your breath. Slowing down and being present with your breath can help you to feel calmer.

* **Be Present.** Whatever you are doing, whether it is the dishes or rocking out at a concert, be completely in it. Being fully present in everything you do, helps you connect with your thoughts and to find joy even in the smallest things.

* **Get Social.** I know this can be difficult but human connection is a key part of what keeps you moving forward. Social connections bring joy, community, meaning, value, and happiness into your life, and they can make a huge difference in your mental health.

✳ **Choose Joy.** Activating joy helps you reconnect with your inner self. It allows you to step away from the world of cancer even if just for a few moments or perhaps even hours. More joy means lower levels of stress in your body, better health, and greater happiness. Choosing joy is choosing to live life right now.

✳ **Work With A Coach.** Working with a coach is one aspect of living in the present. Coaching is designed to help you to uncover what is inside you, and to support you as you focus on moving forward one day at a time. My coaching is a holistic approach that supports people in their body, mind, and spirit as they navigate life with cancer.

Life is meant to be lived in the present. That is why, as they say, it is called a gift. Letting go of the past doesn't mean you have to let go of the beautiful memories you have; it means not staying stuck in the memories that are limiting your ability to move forward. We cannot change the past; it is done, and we cannot live in the future, as it hasn't happened yet. Every opportunity that you take to make life the best it can be right now will help you to see that you can make small changes that make a big difference. Each of these changes will allow you to grow as a person, to see more opportunities to take control of your life, and will keep you in a place of joy and gratitude for what you have right now. This is the beginning of living to thrive with cancer.

Thriver Lessons:

* Be mindful of the past and the future.

* Say "yes" to fun and live right now.

* Living in the present is truly a gift.

Episodes from the

"Living to Thrive with Cancer" Podcast

Fear of Missing Out

Fear of missing out is a real thing for people living with cancer. Explore what you can do to live your best life, and not miss out right now.

Living in the Past, Present, and Future

Staying in the past and projecting into the future is not going to help you move forward in life. Learn why this is important and what you can do to stay present.

Doing the Inner Work

One aspect of the cancer healing process is doing the emotional work that exists on the inside. Learn more about what this means and how you can start doing the inner work.

Feel All the Feels

Healing comes from processing and managing not just your physical health, but also your emotional health. Learn more about processing your emotions so you can feel and release them.

Finding Joy

Joy is an important part of the living with cancer process. Bringing joy into your life will contribute to your overall health and happiness. Learn more about how to bring more joy into your life.

"The secret of health for both mind and body is not to mourn for the past, not to worry about the future, or not to anticipate troubles, but to live in the present moment wisely and earnestly."
—*The Buddha*

Chapter 5

The Family

navigating uncertainty

My husband: Care isn't only the physical and day to day tasks. Care also extends to protecting the emotions of the patient, not just their daily needs. It's deep care.

I must be honest with you – I have been avoiding writing this chapter. Every time I told myself it was time to sit down and start it, I would find something else to do. My go-to emotional response when I am feeling overwhelmed or stressed is the flight response. I want to escape, and in doing so I avoid what is making me uncomfortable. Because I did not like how I was feeling, I kept putting this chapter off. Until now.

Of all the things that I have experienced since my diagnosis, being a wife and mom with cancer has been the most difficult. I can muster the courage for blood work and tests, for surgeries and chemotherapy, but the pain in my heart as I watched and continue to watch my husband and sons navigate my health story is, without a doubt, the most difficult thing I have ever done.

I have experienced the thought that it is me who has created a wound in each of them, that I have damaged our family, and that I took away joy and normal in our life and replaced it with sadness and pain. I know those are my own thoughts and that they aren't completely true but they are real to me, and I need to acknowledge that as part of my healing. Perhaps you have had those thoughts too.

When our boys were little, we would joke about how there is no guide to raising kids – a lot of books, but no specific guide. Our two boys are so different from each other and therefore required different parenting styles. Throw cancer into the mix and it got even more complex. Every family is unique. Every child is unique. Every cancer story is unique. We didn't know how to "do cancer " let alone parent teenagers at the same time. But we did it. It wasn't perfect by any means. Many days it felt like we were making it up as we went along, because in fact - we were.

In all of this, my husband John was trying to hold down the fort. He stepped into the role of caregiver without hesitation as I became focused on what he called my one and only job, and that was to focus on living. We didn't know the statistics of the diagnosis because, as I shared, we chose not to, but we knew that it wasn't good. On the contrary, we chose to focus on the healing, and I focused on myself as best as I could. In doing so, John carried all the burden of everything else. Aside from the medical side of life of which he was completely a part – appointments, tests, surgeries, treatments etc. – John kept the house and our sons moving forward while still going to work at a job that would take him away from home for several days at a time.

This was no small feat, and I admit that I continue to carry the guilt around that burden which he carried, and around my inability to be the mom and wife that I wanted to be.

The Imperfect Process

The medical system does not adequately prepare you for the changes that are about to happen in your life when you receive your cancer diagnosis. They will tell you about the medical stuff, the possible side effects of your treatment, your life expectancy based on the statistics and then send you on your way. I recognize that they are doing their job and that it is not an easy one. Who wants to be the one to tell someone that they have cancer? I also recognize that all doctors are different in their approach and their relationships with their patients. I am just offering that in general, the impact that this has on you and your family is drastically overlooked.

Telling my husband was one thing, but telling our sons was another. How to talk to our sons, and what to tell them became a series of unknowns. We asked ourselves questions like:

How do we tell them I have cancer?

Do we tell them it is stage 4 cancer?

How much detail do we share with them?

What expectations should or shouldn't we have of them?

Is their behaviour because they are teenagers, because I have cancer, or a combination of both?

And, there are so many more that have come up over the years.

Life with cancer is an imperfect process. Every child reacts differently, and the support they need will vary based on their age, personality, and individual circumstances. As a teacher I had some understanding of teenagers and their typical behaviours. It most likely would have been different if the boys had been very young. Age and developmental levels do make a difference in how children think, in what they need, in what they can and cannot do independently, and in how they respond to events. Our expectations of the boys were based on their developmental age and previous expectations.

What we did try to do was to keep things as normal as possible. There were reasonable family and household expectations that existed pre-cancer around helping around the house, doing dishes, tidying up, eating as a family, and being a responsible human being. These did not change because of cancer.

We also supported them in navigating school. Fortunately, they were strong students and continued to do their work. I can imagine it is not like this in all cases, and that some children will need a lot of support to stay present in their own lives.

What I do know from my teaching days, and my now lived experience as a parent with cancer, is that school can be a good place for the child to be. The change of environment, the routine, the friends, and the teachers can make things feel normal, if only for a few hours. We also encouraged our sons to socialise with friends and to continue with extra-curricular activities. I think that this helped them to feel normal, when they really may not have known what they were feeling or how to feel.

At a certain point as routine monitoring revealed recurrences, we chose to stop subjecting our sons to the constant anxiety, which we were experiencing. We could see that some information was manageable for them but too much was very stressful. It became apparent that we had to shield them from unnecessary stress. We had to figure out what the tipping point was. As I tell my coaching clients when it comes to scans and tests, nothing has gone wrong here until we know it has, and then we will deal with it. Based on this we informed the boys of test results after the test, and then from those results we discussed how as a family we would proceed. That is how we chose to handle it. You get to choose what you are going to do.

The Caregiver

Like managing children, navigating your relationship with your spouse or partner is also an imperfect process. The challenges after a diagnosis really tests a couples' ability to manage in the face of adversity. There will be moments of extreme emotion in both parties. Fear around this life changing event can manifest as anger that this is even happening. Grief around having cancer and all the pain it causes can present as distancing to try to avoid the situation. Joyful moments can be stolen by sadness of the potential lost future moments. When I started cancer coaching, I was quite surprised to learn that not every partner is supportive throughout the process. It is understandable as this situation tests your relationship with each other, "in sickness and in health…" and in your relationship with yourself. Whomever the caregiver is, whether they are a friend, a loved one, an adult child, or a partner, there is a tremendous responsibility taken on when you commit to this role.

For National Caregivers Day I interviewed my husband on my podcast. It was a very poignant interview because it was unscripted and addressed our real-life situation. This was the first time that we had publicly put ourselves out there and expressed what our reality actually looked like. From the outside we looked like we had it all together, but in reality, we were just managing day by day. John has recently admitted that, if we were to do the podcast interview again, he would add so much more to the conversation. What he wanted to share with the listeners were the thoughts inside his head that naturally occur with a caregiver spouse, the ones he dared not say out loud, the terrifying thoughts that made him think about negative outcomes and "what am I going to do if..." thoughts that gave him shame for even contemplating. I believe that these thoughts are so normal.

What he did express in our podcast episode was that care isn't only the physical and day to day tasks. Care also extends to protecting the emotions of the patient, not just their daily needs. It's deep care. Even in the interview he was protecting me by withholding his deepest fears and the resulting trauma that he continues to experience because of cancer coming into our life. John is aware that he must push these thoughts out of his mind as he carries his own fear and trauma.

While the cancer patient is experiencing emotional and physical consequences, so too is the caregiver. There are so many demands on them that often their own needs are put aside – time for themselves, time out with friends, personal interests, intimacy – a list of losses that may go unnoticed by others. A caregiver may not even see that they are grieving, and subsequently their own needs drop by the wayside. What falls on the caregiver is the day-to-day management of the patient's needs, the family dynamics, the functioning of the house, the appointments, and they still have their own work responsibilities. People often offer help but how do you ask for support when you don't know what you need? Caregivers are juggling life just trying to keep all the balls in the air often to the detriment of their own well-being. So, the question is, if the caregiver is helping the patient, who is helping the caregiver?

Time to Heal

I recently asked my now adult children for their thoughts on what it looked like for them as teenagers of a mom with cancer. What I got from them was not what I expected. I don't know if I knew exactly what to expect, and perhaps I shouldn't be surprised by their responses.

My request opened a Pandora's box of pain, grief, anger, and honesty, but most importantly, it opened the door for each of us to look at our own healing and where we are on that path. Opening that box has created some big conversations – between my two sons, between the boys and their dad, between the boys and myself, and between my husband and me. As a family we are only now healing because we are ready to have the conversations and talk about what happened.

Both boys wrote me a letter expressing their thoughts and feelings. Out of respect for them, I will not share what they wrote but here is what we learned... *Healing is a very individual process.*

My husband and I have reflected a lot on how we have navigated the years since my diagnosis. No doubt we made a lot of mistakes. How can you not when there is no specific guide that can address every big or small issue, every emotion, and every decision that has to be made. Our sons may not have felt at the time as they do now since time and maturity have allowed them to reflect and process what they could not then. However, I want to recognize and honour that they did the best that they could with what they had to work with. Their love and support made a difference for all of us. It wasn't perfect, but as much as they could have completely rebelled and added an even more complex layer to the story, they didn't. At least not in big ways. Their small rebellions were to be expected and were manageable. I am grateful for them and their strength and compassion.

Not every family is going to experience cancer like we did. I wish there was a clear and specific guide of steps to success but there isn't. Like the patient's cancer story, this is a unique situation, and it is going to be different for each family. These are some key takeaways from our experience. You may find them helpful.

* **Tell People You Need Help**. It takes a village to raise a child, more so when a parent is ill and cannot be present for their child. It takes courage for the caregiver to ask for help, especially when you don't know what you need. You can't and don't have to figure everything out alone. Others may offer insights that you don't have and solutions that you can't see.

* **Ask Family To Check In.** We did not do this because we assumed they just would. Family check ins would have helped our sons and given them support that we couldn't and allowed my husband the chance to choose if he wanted to get support. Extended family can bring comfort and

distraction to a child. Getting both the child and the caregiver out of the house and giving them a break from what is happening to the patient, can allow them space to breathe and perhaps even share how they are really feeling.

* **Kids And Caregivers Need Support.** Our teenagers were able to hide their feelings during therapist visits. They were not interested in sharing with someone they didn't know or trust. Children need to be ready to talk. There needs to be support in place so that they can process the emotions and confusion they are experiencing. The same can be said for the caregiver. They need time to rest away from their partner, to share their thoughts and feelings, and to be heard. Support needs to be in place for the entire family, not just the person with cancer.

* **Spend Time Together.** Allow each family member to choose something that they want to do and put it on the calendar. We had Mandatory Family Fun Days. It was just the four of us, and we did things to step away from the cancer narrative and to make lasting memories.

✳ **Know Your Kids.** They need to know just enough that they aren't wondering what is happening. Tell them what you think they can handle, but perhaps not all the details. This is unique to each family and each family is unique.

✳ **Let Them Ask Questions.** Kids are smart and they are curious. Allowing them space to ask questions allows them to decide what they want to know, and what they need to know. It gives them some control when they are likely feeling quite helpless.

The Unexpected Gift

Something happened to our family because of cancer. We changed. Each of us has gone through our personal ups and downs, joys and pains, grief and celebration, in our own way. The life I live with cancer has changed me as a person. I am kinder, more compassionate, less angry at the world, and gentler with myself. I see changes in my family as well. Each of them has, whether consciously or not, learned from this and made positive changes in their own lives. One of the greatest successes that we are grateful for is that in all of this, when we could have all pushed back and gone our separate ways, we instead stepped in and became closer.

We are a family that can now have big conversations, a family that can question each other from a place of love, and we are a family that communicates more openly and honestly than we ever did before.

During one of our many conversations around this topic my husband said to me, "Isn't it beautiful that we can even have conversations like this." The beauty lies in two things: we and our sons are ready and able to have this conversation, and I am still here to be part of it.

Thriver Lessons:

* Do your best as a family.

* Tell people to check on your family.

* You can grow together when you share.

Episodes from the

"Living to Thrive with Cancer" Podcast

<u>Caregivers the Unsung Heroes</u>

Caregivers play a very important role in a patient's life with cancer. They are the unsung heroes. Listen to an interview with my husband to talk about what life looks like during cancer, from the caregiver's perspective.

<u>Three Strategies to Support Your Family</u>

Learn three things we did as a family that helped us to navigate my stage 4 colon cancer diagnosis. This could help you if you are struggling with the family dynamic and how to navigate cancer at your house.

"To us, family means putting your arms around each other and being there."

- Barbara Bush

Chapter 6

The Scars We Carry

inside and out

Me to my husband: Is that man looking at my scars?

My husband: If he is, he is either curious about what happened, or he is thinking how strong you are because he knows what you have been through.

I am grateful for my body. This may not be what you would expect to hear from a stage 4 cancer thriver who has had six surgeries, but it is true. A different version of me would be embarrassed, ashamed, or even angry and resentful, hating the scars that cover my abdomen, mark my back, and live in my soul. I am scarred both inside and outside.

My physical scars look back at me every time I am near a mirror. I feel their tightness when I move. They cover my entire upper abdomen in a series of lines that are a different colour and texture. Laying alongside my navel, there are three scars – one is a large hook shape from my colon surgery. It runs vertically from above my belly button to a few inches below. The other two shorter permanent markings lie adjacent to the large one.

On my abdomen, from my liver resection surgery, there is a very large upside down V shaped scar. It is the size of my open hand, and runs from under my right rib cage pointing upwards to just below my sternum and back down to my left rib cage. My two separate lung metastasis resection surgeries left me with a large fish hook shaped scar that runs along the entire length under my right shoulder blade. On my left rib cage under my bra line are three large scars. In addition to these, the port-a-cath and surgery drain hose scars appear on various other parts of my torso.

Six surgeries in under nine years have left a multitude of scars across my body. Some of them occasionally ache deeply into the tissue beneath. Some have no feeling at all as the nerve damage has left me numb to all feelings of touch in the area. Those are the scars you can see. What you cannot see are the emotional scars.

Your Scars Are Not Just Surface Wounds

One of the pieces that I believe is missing from medical treatment plans is the after care. I wish that someone had told me what I should do to help my body get strong again; instead, I had to figure it out on my own.

Healing after treatment is an entirely different type of work. It can still fall under the scope of medical care, but there are also holistic therapies that you can access during and after your treatment process, if it is safe and available.

Scars aren't just funky looking wounds that have healed. Scars actually have a significant impact on the workings of your body. Scar tissue may cause pain in several ways. Sometimes, the pain is due to skin tightness, which may make it difficult to move freely, while in other cases, scar tissue pain occurs due to nerve damage resulting from the original injury. If the wound was deep and affected nerves or tendons, a person might have long-term symptoms. This is why post treatment management of scars is so important.

Nurturing Your Physical Scars

Taking care of your scars can help to heal your body, and allow you to regain mobility and range of motion. Rubbing a chemical-free skin care oil on your healed scar can help to reduce itching and promote fading. Massage can break down the collagen fibres and scar tissue to promote healing through improved blood circulation, which promotes tissue regeneration. This can allow for greater range of motion in the body that may have been lost post-surgery. Caring for your scars can not only improve their appearance, but it may also improve your emotional well-being and quality of life.

The Unseen Wounds

The emotional toll that cancer takes on a person is often not talked about. Cancer is such a physical condition happening in the body, but with it comes wounds that are internal, emotional scars. These emotional scars show up in many different forms, often unexpectedly, and they can be very powerful.

Three years after I was done treatments, I could feel that there was still something missing in my healing process. I experienced confusion around the joy of being a survivor, and the ongoing fear of the future.

I would burst into tears at a song one minute, and be celebrating life the next. Although I was rebuilding my life and feeling grateful to be alive, my soul still felt empty.

Nurturing Your Emotional Scars

It is important to talk about how to move forward after a diagnosis. It is a gross understatement to say that cancer causes trauma. These internal scars are related to the emotional part of healing. You may not see the trauma on the outside, but it is holding a space inside that feels heavy and sad. It is fear, anger, confusion, acute stress, trauma, emotional triggers, and more. It can be debilitating and often overlooked. Each of you is going to respond to trauma differently based on your circumstances. What is important is that you learn to identify the trauma and seek tools to support yourself.

All of my clients express the emotional toll that cancer has had on their body due to the emphasis that society places on physical appearances. They believe that they will stand out as looking different and will be judged by others. I have had clients tell me that they won't wear clothes that reveal their scars because they are ashamed of their appearance. They are afraid people will ask them what happened, and they fear the questions will bring up trauma and pain they don't want to feel. Instead, they cover themselves up physically and emotionally.

One client shared that she struggles with wearing pretty underwear because of her scars and how she feels about her body. Another shared that intimacy is a problem because radiation left her pelvic region scarred and tight. Another shared that her husband struggles with her appearance because of her mastectomy and lack of nipples. Others speak about the neuropathy that affects their hands and feet, their loss of hair from treatment, and the ostomy bag that keeps them home because they fear that it will leak in public.

I have heard stories of women who want their ostomies reversed to regain their freedom, while at the same time being afraid that their bowels won't remember how to function leaving them incontinent. These are real concerns from real women whose emotional health is directly impacted by their physical self. Their thoughts surrounding their body image manifests as feelings of diminished self-worth.

Another effect that cancer treatment has on the body is memory function. My clients experience a lack of mental sharpness or mental fog. This is known as

Chemo Brain. It is a common side effect of treatment that others cannot see and that can be difficult to explain. It is different in its symptoms and severity for everyone. Long and short term memory issues can leave you feeling uncomfortable in conversations, afraid to return to work, and insecure around others. Memory impairment is an emotional scar that can leave you struggling to manage and to feel normal.

Mental health interventions need to be in place from the moment of diagnosis, throughout the treatment process, and into the post treatment years. Cancer is addressed as a physical illness, but I would argue that of equal importance are the emotional and mental health needs of the patient.

If you feel overwhelmed or aren't sure how to move forward, I am pleased you are reading this book. Seek help. You don't have to do this alone.

Quotes About Scars That May Bring You Peace

"Scars are beautiful when we see them as glorious reminders that we have courageously survived."
— *Lysa TerKeurst*

"Some people see scars and it is wounding they remember. To me they are proof of the fact that there is healing."
— *Linda Hogan*

"Your scars are someone else's signs of hope."
— *Danielle Laporte*

"Scars show us where we have been, they do not dictate where we are going."
— *David Rossi*

Thriver Lessons:

* Your scars mean you are still here.

* Get support for the emotional scars.

* There is no shame in having scars.

Episodes from the

"Living to Thrive with Cancer" Podcast

Body Image and Cancer

Cancer thrivers who have had surgeries that have resulted in scarring or visible changes in the body may wonder how to navigate clothes, gatherings, and the public. There are a lot of thoughts and feelings that go hand in hand with your new body and what you can do to support it.

Building Your Personal Health Care Team

For people living with cancer, having care outside of the medical world is key. Having a personal health care team in place is a great way to nurture your body, mind, and spirit.

Memory and Focus

If you have had cancer then it is quite likely that you have also experienced memory and focus issues. Living with cancer brings its own challenges, but you can work to overcome them. Learn strategies to manage memory issues and tools to support you in the process.

The Impact of Cancer

Cancer has an emotional and mental impact on your life. Cancer survivors cannot take the emotional and mental health impact of cancer lightly. It is physically life changing, which is the part that everyone sees, but there is a lot underneath and behind the scars.

"When I look at my scars, they are my daily reminder that I have work to do and it is the best work of my life - taking care of myself."
– Kathryn White

Chapter 7

The Things That Set You Off

resolving stress

Person: My third cousin died of colon cancer.
Me: This is not helpful.

Even as I write this, I can feel my emotions being activated. There is an energy moving in me. It is a slow welling up of a vibration that starts at my heart and radiates through my body. I must stop what I am doing to breathe because the urge to fight or flee is coursing through me. Next come the tears that I cannot always explain, and that aren't always attached to any specific memory. Sometimes the tears are an overwhelming emotional response to my trauma. My brain feels foggy, and I have to give myself grace as I refocus and try to keep moving forward. This is a difficult feeling to explain, to quantify, and to rationalise. It is my brain wanting to keep me safe even when I am not actively afraid. This is a trigger and, in this case, it is reflecting on this very topic that is setting me off.

A trigger is a stimulus, such as a situation, word, or even a memory, that elicits a strong emotional response that is often negative. It can include sights, smells, sounds and certain locations. This response can activate feelings of anger, sadness, fear, or anxiety. Triggers are often linked to past experiences, particularly those that were traumatic or deeply impactful. They can cause a person to relive emotions, sometimes intensely, and often unexpectedly. Recognizing your triggers can be important for managing emotional responses, and improving your mental well-being.

An emotional response can come from something as simple as the machine that pings when your IV bag is empty. The sound of the ping alone can elicit a fight or flight response.

Another trigger may be related to music. Certain songs, perhaps songs that were played during the time that you were in treatment, or songs that remind you of your life before cancer can bring up tears, or rage, or grief. Movies, books, and TV programs that have a plot line or even a reference to cancer, may make you resent the show and take away your joy. It will be different for each of you based on your own experiences. Below are strategies you can try when you are experiencing a trigger.

* **Acknowledge what you are feeling**. Being aware of your response will allow you to navigate it. Name what you are feeling but don't own it.

* **Ask yourself why.** The trigger is coming from inside you and your memory. Being able to identify why you are having a response can help you process the emotions tied to it, work through healing the memory of the event, and allow you some control moving forward.

* **Breathe.** In the moment it may feel like you can't control what is happening. Put one hand on your chest and one hand on your belly. Inhale and exhale. Very slowly and very deeply. Feel your belly and chest rise and fall. Your exhale helps to engage the rest and reset response in your nervous system. Keep breathing until you feel the trigger slipping away and calm returning.

* **Get Grounded.** There are several ways to get grounded. You can place your feet on the floor, maybe even taking off your shoes. You can lie down on the floor or on the ground to connect your whole body with the earth. Standing in water or allowing water to run over your hands can feel calming. The objective is to have a surface that you can feel and connect to so that you can be present, not in the trigger.

* **Do a sensory check in.** Scan through all of your senses. What do you see? Is there a smell? What can you hear or taste? What do you feel under your hands or feet? Connecting with your senses helps to support being present and aware of right now, not the event of the past.

* **Five things you can see.** Look around your space. Find five things you can see and name them out loud. This is another way to be in the present as you see what is in your space. Repeat this as many times as you need to.

It is important to note that caregivers can experience strong triggers as well. My husband, as my caregiver, cannot bear the smell of disinfectant wipes. His brain associates that smell with the hospital, and it sends him to a place that he doesn't want to remember. He struggles when driving past the hospital. The building alone haunts him with memories of watching me wheeled away for surgery not knowing what the outcome would be, sitting for hours waiting for the surgeon to appear, and having to leave me to go home to our sons and at times an empty house.

None of our personal triggers are more important than another. Our triggers are unique to us based on our personal experiences and how our brain responds to them.

Your brain is very powerful and it holds on to memories to protect you from danger. Each response is the brain stepping in to protect you from perceived danger, while it ironically takes you back to those memories that are so painful. I can honestly say that we were not prepared for the emotional fallout that we would experience from cancer. I'm not sure that anything can.

The Unconscious

Moving on after cancer may seem straightforward to the people around you. They may feel that the procedure and process are done, so now you can leave it all behind and go back to your life. This is a common issue that my clients bring to our calls. They talk about how people don't understand what they have been through, and that they expect them to be okay now. Frustrations emerge around how friends and family assume they will want to go back to work to leave all the cancer stuff behind. They feel angry when everyone tells them how good they look, and that they don't even look like they have been sick. Meanwhile, despite what others think, they are still trying to manage side effects that keep them feeling unwell.

Another common issue that arises is that friends and family sometimes feel the need to share anecdotes of others who have cancer and those who have died. I used to get so angry when people would say these things that I considered to be cruel. I wondered how they could possibly think that a death story or a long-drawn-out account of someone else's treatment and pain could be helpful or comforting to me. Every story they shared made me project myself into the person they were talking about.

To protect ourselves from these unwanted stories, we had to come up with a strategy. We had a chalkboard hung outside our front door. My husband was so frustrated with the insensitive stories and comments entering our household that he wrote the following on this chalkboard: *"Positivity only. Check your negativity at the door."*

This served as a message that we would not allow any negative stories to influence our lives. Perhaps we offended some, perhaps we pushed some people away. I would say that was not our problem, as we were trying to keep our life together and needed to be lifted up, not brought down. This is one of the choices you get to make when you take control of your life.

Perhaps you have encountered these people and struggled with how to manage these conversations. You may feel triggered by what they are sharing as it takes you back into your story. You may want to stop the person or change the subject but don't know how. The question is why does this even happen in the first place?

When I was in treatment, I went to speak to my minister who also had cancer. I asked her about these people and how they could be so insensitive. She said that she had started to call them "the unconscious". She reasoned that because of their own lack of personal experience with cancer that they weren't conscious or even aware of the pain their words were causing. This made sense to me, but it still didn't help me to resolve how I felt about their lack of compassion. It was after becoming a holistic cancer coach and navigating this question so many times with my clients that a thought occurred to me that has made all the difference in my view of others and for my clients.

My reasoning comes down to human nature. As humans we seek ways to make connections with other people. In making connections we can find something in common that will allow us to start to build a relationship. When people hear that you have cancer, unless they have had it themselves, they don't get it. They don't have the internal understanding of the physical and emotional pain you endure and so, they respond in a way that gives them something in common with you – a cancer story. I believe in my heart that people are not inherently cruel, but they just want to connect, and given how we are socialized to believe that cancer is a death sentence, when they don't know what to say, they revert to finding common ground, which is often a story of someone they know with cancer. This belief has allowed me to release anger towards these people, and has given me the courage to take back control and stop their story in its tracks to protect myself. Your mental health is of the utmost importance. Your emotional scars need to be cared for and supported.

Getting Through the Tough Stuff

I wish I knew then what I know now; you can get through the tough stuff when you know what to do to support yourself. What you are experiencing may bring you to your knees or you may tuck away what you are feeling while you just do what you have to do to get through this. Each cancer survivor is going to have their own way of coping with the things they fear like tests, scans, and even reoccurrence.

Post treatment, I continue to have routine scans for monitoring. Until a few years ago, prior to a scan there was a notable shift in our family dynamic. I would start to get quiet and distant; my husband would get hyper attentive to my needs and constantly check in on how I was feeling. We would have little arguments, which was uncommon for us. It was like we were dancing around each other avoiding something that we couldn't quite name. What we didn't realise was that in the days and weeks before the upcoming scan, we were in fight or flight mode. We were having the anxiety that many cancer survivors call "scanxiety".

Once we realised what was happening, we were able to talk about it and share our feelings with each other.

This led me to learn how to manage my own anxiety, and eventually to create a process I call AIDE.

AIDE is an acronym. It is a tool that I give my clients to help them when they are feeling overwhelmed, anxious or afraid. This tool helps you to self-regulate what you are experiencing and to support yourself as you move into, through, and beyond whatever is elevating your emotions. I want to share this tool with you so that you can also learn how to get through the tough stuff.

AIDE Stress Management Tool

A – *address the thought*

Everything we experience begins with a thought. Some I call sneaky thoughts – they appear when you least expect them and can stop you in your tracks. This is why I believe that managing your mindset is such an important part of the cancer process. Address the thought by seeing and hearing what is coming into your mind. What are you thinking? Why are you thinking it? Is it a real thought or is your fight or flight response creating fear?

By learning how to notice what it is that is challenging you, you can learn to control it, and perhaps even stop it. This will help you in many situations. Start by addressing the thought.

I – *invite in the breath*

Thoughts are going to activate your sympathetic nervous system, sending you into fight or flight and raising your stress hormone, cortisol. When you breathe fully and deeply you are slowing yourself, your mind, and your breath down. The exhale of a breath activates the parasympathetic response which is the rest and digest response. When you move into rest and digest, your body starts to go back to homeostasis or home, the place where it feels safe again. In this state, your cortisol levels come down, and the stress response releases.

If you find yourself triggered, or overwhelmed by fear, try this – put your left hand on your heart and your right hand on your belly. Take an inhale and say a mantra to yourself, (ex. "I am safe") then exhale with the same or a different mantra (ex. "I am calm").

Repeat this as many times as you need to. You can always leave out the hand placement if that does not feel comfortable for you. The nice thing about using your breath is that nobody needs to know you are even doing it. It is a private practice just for you.

D - *decide the outcome*

You and I both know that the outcome of a test is not within your control, but what you can control is how you approach it. You can decide how you want the process to go. For example, if you are going for a scan you can decide to believe that everything will be okay. Of course, you don't know what the outcome will be until you are told, but by telling yourself that it is going to be okay, you are supporting calm in your body, and telling your mind that you don't want to hear the negative stories that it wants to tell you. This is a form of reframing your thoughts. Self-belief is so important in your cancer story. If this feels like too much, then decide that you are going to feel calm and confident going into the scan. Come back to the breath if your emotions and thoughts start to run away on you. Believe that you can do this. Tell yourself you can do this and then do it.

E – *envision the process*

Visualisation is a very powerful tool. I have found that when I picture what is going to happen on the day of an appointment, test, or surgery, I can manage easier. This process can even start before the day of the appointment. For example, if your test is at the hospital, picture everything leading up to getting to the hospital. See yourself getting out of bed and walking yourself through your morning routine (Perhaps you even have a day of a procedure routine in place already). Imagine you doing everything from eating, to brushing your teeth, to getting in the car and driving to your appointment. Picture your drive, what route you will take, what you will see along the way and how long it will take. See yourself parking, walking into the appointment, and going to the check in. Go through every step along the way including getting changed, going into the space and getting ready for the scan or test. Picture yourself receiving the scan and practise the mantra you have chosen as you go through the process. My favourite mantra to say during a scan is "I am happy, I am healthy". Then, go through the reverse process once the scan is done. Envision being finished, leaving the appointment, and going home or to a place that brings you joy.

This may take some practice, but what I have found is that it mentally prepares me for what is coming, and it allows me to control how I see and perceive myself in that moment.

I remember the first-time post-surgery that I wore a two-piece bathing suit in public. My husband and I were on vacation at a thermal spa in Germany and we were heading to the pool. The irony was that this spa would have left most North Americans feeling a little self-conscious. When we walked on to the deck, there were so many people all doing their own thing, yet I felt like all eyes were on me. I noticed a man looking in my direction and thought to myself that he must be looking at my scars. I asked my husband if he thought the man was looking at me and he replied, *"No, but if he is, he is either curious about what happened or he is thinking how strong you are because he knows what you have been through."*

It was such a silly thought but it shows where I was in my healing process – self-conscious and self-aware. I am no longer worried if people see my scars. They are a badge of honour for me, a reminder that I have faced challenges I never thought I would, and that I am still here. When I look down at my abdomen, I see a large V shape that my husband says stands for VICTORY.

The physical and emotional scars are a daily reminder to stay on my path to health and to do everything I can to avoid the downward slope on the path towards disease. I have stopped feeling resentful and instead am grateful for my life. Instead of viewing this new me as an effort, I have found ease in accepting and managing this new version of myself.

In the midst of trying to navigate life with cancer, I want to offer you a thought – give yourself grace. This is hard work. Be gentle with yourself, patient with your physical and emotional self, and ask for help to support your healing.

Thriver Lessons:

* Navigating triggers makes a difference.

* Words have an impact.

* You can learn how to manage scanxiety.

Episodes from the

"Living to Thrive with Cancer" Podcast

<u>What Nobody Tells You About Healing</u>

Healing isn't in the moment; deep healing comes after all the medication, treatments, and plans are done. Deep healing takes time.

<u>Reframing Adversity</u>

Cancer is a source of profound adversity in your life. It requires you to face situations that you never expected, to do things you never imagined having to do, and to face terrifying realities. From adversity can come resiliency. Learn how to reframe adversity in order to support yourself in your life with cancer.

Every day brings a choice: to practise
stress or to practise peace.

- Joan Borysenko

Chapter 8

Rebuild Your Foundation

eating healthy and moving your body

Me to my medical team: So what should
I eat while I'm on treatment?
Medical team: Anything you want,
anything you can keep down.
Me to myself: That's your best answer? Seriously?

I honestly thought that part of my cancer treatment plan would include education on a healthy lifestyle and how to support my body during the process. What surprised me was not just the lack of information I received but the fact that I was left to figure it out on my own. I now know that there were resources available, but amidst the overwhelming diagnosis, navigating surgery and treatment, and honestly just trying to survive, I wasn't mentally or physically able to go searching.

Looking back, I remember being handed a big binder of information on our first visit to the oncologist. Buried at the back was a brief list of places to contact, websites to visit, and various other types of possible support. I was barely able to wrap my brain around what was happening in my life, so the binder was overwhelming, scary, and felt like an invitation to figure it out myself.

Some of my clients are fully committed to exploring and learning how to support their bodies through diving into researching their diagnosis and alternative modalities. This is how they move into action. Many others share the same sentiment about that binder – that it was just another layer on an already heavy burden. What they really desire is someone to guide them, eliminate confusion, and help them initiate small changes that can make a big difference. There is no right or wrong way. There is the way that feels right for you and that you can manage without feeling overwhelmed and fearful. Peace of mind comes in many different forms.

The work that I am sharing here began the year after my first two surgeries and chemotherapy. I knew I needed to heal my body, nourish it, and rebuild my strength. At the suggestion of a friend, I took a nutrition course that changed my life forever. This is where I learned about the power of food. From this space I started a business of teaching women in my community how to create simple healthy meals that would support their health and healing. We would gather in my kitchen and I would cook for them while explaining the health building benefits of what I was creating. Then we would sit together and enjoy the dishes I had prepared and talk about topics that were important to them.

A few years later I felt like something was still missing in my life and in my soul. I signed up for a yoga teacher-training program that showed me the importance of movement for personal and emotional healing. This was where the desire and determination to learn more and to bring holistic healing into my life began.

From here my business evolved as I continued to share what I had learned about food and I started to teach yoga classes in my community. I knew I was on a path towards something bigger, I just wasn't there yet.

Everything You Put In Your Body Matters

Bringing healthy eating habits into your life is the foundation of caring for your body. Think of your health as a slope. On one end of the slope is good health and on the other end is disease… or a state of "dis-ease".

When your body is out of alignment with its natural state of health it is moving down the slope towards dis-ease, which ultimately can lead to a medical condition. Being aware of, and changing what you put in and on your body, will move you towards good health and away from dis-ease. Unfortunately, this is not how much of society thinks when it comes to our health.

Our society is built on a "get-things-quick-and-easy" mentality. This includes what we eat. Convenience comes at a price. Quick and easy foods are generally not health-building. They are moving you towards the disease end of the path. Building a healthy body requires you to rethink what foods you are eating and to create a different relationship with food. This can be very difficult if you haven't previously thought about the power of food and how it matters in your life.

You are surrounded by choices every day when it comes to food - fast food that you don't even have to leave your car or even your home to have delivered to you, food that is made from cheap ingredients with little to no nutritional value, and food that is created to sell, not to support your health. Because everything you put in your body matters, it is important that you start to be aware of the difference between health-building and disease-building foods.

Health Building Foods

Let's start with the difference between how you eat and what you eat. There are a lot of styles of eating available to you that may be recommended: vegan, vegetarian, paleo, pescatarian, alkaline, keto, and more. I am not here to tell you how to eat; I want to guide you on what to eat. The answer is simple: Eat whole foods. Eat mostly plants.

I like to follow three rules. The first is to eat organic if you can. The Environmental Working Group publishes a list every year of the Dirty Dozen and the Clean Fifteen. These lists outline the fruits and vegetables that carry the highest and lowest loads of pesticides.

The Dirty Dozen is a great place to start if you are able to purchase organic foods. These are the foods that you want to buy organic, such as strawberries, spinach, and peaches. The Clean Fifteen can be your guide if organic is not available to you. Examples include avocados, onions, and mushrooms. You can visit www.ewg.org for the most up to date lists.

My next rule is to eat as locally as possible. This will allow you to know where your food is coming from, and you can even get to know the farmer if you buy straight from the source. Your local farmer's market is the perfect place to build relationships around food and to know the source of your fruits and vegetables, and even your grains and meat.

My third rule is to eat in season. The fruits and vegetables that are consumed during their ideal season, and closer to harvest, will contain a higher quantity of nutrients, which is what your body needs when you are supporting your immune system and healing. Eating in season can also be less expensive. Another option is to eat frozen fruits and vegetables. They are still high in nutrients and also are less expensive to buy than fresh, especially during the off season. Frozen vegetables are typically frozen in their prime state.

Whole foods are foods that come straight from the source. They are fresh fruits and vegetables, clean meats, whole grains, nuts and seeds, beans and legumes, and healthy oils like olive oil, avocado oil, and coconut oil.

These foods have not gone through chemical alteration in a lab and have not had additives, preservatives, or food colouring added to them. They are foods that have not been stripped of their nutrients and then re-infused with synthesised nutrients. They are just food. This is what you need to be eating. These are the foods that are going to support your cells, your organs, your muscles, your energy, and your immune system.

Plant-Based Eating

Plant-based eating is centred around meals that are mostly plants. Typically, in North America, we have it backwards. Meat is often the biggest portion on our dinner plates. This isn't to say that meat isn't good for you. However, meat has become the focus of our eating, meaning that plants have taken the back seat. Fruits and vegetables, beans, grains, and legumes are full of vitamins and phytonutrients - nutrients that aren't in meat but that your body needs. This doesn't mean you can't eat meat, you just need to eat mostly plants.

The Benefits of a Plant-Based Diet

When you have cancer and when you are recovering from surgeries, treatments, and the entire process in general, it is important to know how to support your body. Eating a plant-based diet has a number of benefits including the following.

* **Boosting Your Immune System.** Your immune system is a complex network of cells and organs that constantly fights disease, illness, and infection. It works hard and needs to be replenished. To do this, try to make two-thirds of each meal vegetables, fruits, and whole grains. These foods contain valuable antioxidants and phytonutrients, which your body uses to keep you healthy. Make one-third of your meals lean protein like chicken, fish, or plant proteins such as beans or quinoa. An immune system that is being built up will help you to fight off infections and support your systems. You want to have a strong immune system that is ready when you need it.

* **Reducing Inflammation.** Not all inflammation is bad. Inflammation is a protective response of the body to fight infections, repair tissues, and heal itself after injury. However, if this inflammation persists in the body and becomes chronic, it can negatively impact your health. Plants are loaded with phytonutrients, many of which have anti-inflammatory properties

that may help the body heal more quickly and stop inflammation. The key aspect of reducing inflammation in your body isn't just what you put in it; it is what you don't put in it.

✳ **Increasing Fibre Intake.** Eating foods that contain fibre and are plant-based improves the health of your gut so you are better able to absorb the nutrients from food that support your immune system while reducing inflammation. Fibre can also stabilise your blood sugar and support your elimination system. As well, fibre cleans your colon, acting like a scrub brush. This helps clean out bacteria and other buildup in your intestines. You need the fibre from plants and whole grains in your diet.

Disease Building Foods

In sharp contrast to the health-building foods are the foods that most of our society eats. These are the foods that are easy to access, inexpensive, and convenient. These are the foods in the Standard American (SAD) or Western Diet. These are the foods that are highly marketed, often with disclaimers on the labels of how healthy they are to make you want to buy them. These are the foods that are moving you away from good health. They are highly refined and they contain few nutrients. They are infused with chemicals to make them shelf-stable so they don't go bad quickly. Colouring and flavouring are added to them to make them look and taste better. They are packed with unhealthy oils and refined sugars, which are sources of inflammation, and have little to no nutritional value.

To support your body throughout the cancer process and beyond, you need to make changes to what you put in your body. If you already avoid highly processed, nutrient-depleted foods, this is great! If you don't, then it is time to start making some changes that will make a difference on your path towards good health. I cannot say it enough: everything you put in your body matters. This may feel like a big and overwhelming task, but I know you can do it. Choose health building, which includes getting rid of foods that don't support your body, and instead bringing in foods that will build you up and create an environment where your health can grow.

A Word About Water

Water is a key part of supporting your body. In contrast to water are sugary drinks. It is important for you to know that sugary drinks, including energy drinks and pop, are part of a disease building lifestyle. What your body really needs is water. It is the thing that you can easily add to your daily life that can make a difference.

The bodily systems need water, which supports the regulation of body temperature, the transportation of nutrients and oxygen into the cells, and the supporting of the joints. Water helps with the absorption of nutrients, helps with eliminating waste from the body, supports brain function, and so much more.

Don't like water? Make it fun by adding frozen fruit, mint, lemon, or cucumber. What is important is to reduce sugar intake to help decrease inflammation and to increase water intake to support moving you up the path towards health.

Never Eat Anything You Can't Pronounce

Think of your body as a periodic table, like the one you learned in high school science. On this table are many forms of elements that exist in our world. Your body is its own little world and is also made up of elements such as calcium, magnesium, and potassium. These are health-supportive elements that need to be replaced as they are used up. They need to be replaced with whole foods that are full of nutrients, not chemicals.

When you look at a package of food, take a moment to read the ingredients label. The ingredients are in order of quantity in the food. The first ingredient is the highest ingredient, while the last is the lowest ingredient. So, if sugar is the third thing on the list, then you know that sugar is the third highest ingredient in that food. Also, take a moment to read the ingredients out loud. Typically, on processed food labels, there are words that feel like they came from a science lesson. They are long, complicated, and difficult to pronounce. Those are typically the additives and preservatives that are not natural whole foods. As the old saying goes, "Never eat anything you can't pronounce… except quinoa, you should always eat quinoa." It's pronounced keen-wah.

Get Moving

Another aspect of our lives that is moving us towards the disease end of the path is how little we actually move our bodies. We are not designed to sit all day. Regular movement, through whatever type of exercise feels good for you, is key to your overall health, whether you have cancer or not.

I remember one day when I was still in treatment, I had the urge to go for a run. Before cancer, I had been a marathoner. Sitting on the couch supported rest, but it didn't feel good in my body. My body wanted to move and it felt called to go for a run. I knew it would be a short run, and I knew it would be a slow run. I was so proud of myself for strapping on my shoes and slowly trotting down our street. About two minutes into my run a car pulled over, and my friends hopped out. They were appalled that I was running. They exclaimed that I should be at home resting, that this was too much for my body, and that I needed to stop.

They were wrong. Even in treatment, your body can move, and it needs to move. Exercise helps not just with your physical health but also your mental health. There are studies that show that people who exercise while they are receiving cancer treatments respond better to their treatment plan.

In one of my podcast episodes I interviewed Coral Levkovitz, MS, MD/MBA student, who helped to facilitate a study on women who exercised while they were in chemotherapy for breast cancer. What they discovered was that the women not only felt better, but they enjoyed the challenge within themselves to continue exercising after the study was over, and they had improved mental health.

My movement of choice has become yoga. I don't view it as exercise; I view it as a lifestyle. Yoga allows me to move and stretch my body in ways that feel good for me. There are so many types of yoga to choose from. What I also like about yoga is how it supports mental health. Slowing down, connecting with the breath, and being present, allows the body to come back to homeostasis or home. It is like a reset for your body and soul.

Trusting yourself and knowing what is right for you is an important part of life with cancer. Get curious about what you can do to move your body. There are so many options including yoga, swimming, walking, tai chi, pickle-ball, and more. When you learn how to listen to your body, you will hear what it wants. This is your opportunity to say yes to fun, to try something new, and to support your health-building life while trusting yourself and caring for yourself.

Lifestyle Changes Matter

What you put in your body will make a difference in your overall health. Whole foods will not just support you on a cellular level; they will also help to increase your energy. Food is energy. It fuels your body and allows you to do the things you want to be doing. Moving your body will also help you to build energy. Sitting makes you want to sit more. It becomes a habit, and then a lifestyle. It depletes your energy. Healthy food, exercise, and movement don't just support your cells and muscles, they also support your hormones.

Your hormones regulate everything in your body. Serotonin plays a key role in body functions like mood, sleep, digestion, nausea, wound healing, bone health, blood clotting, and more. Dopamine gives you feelings of pleasure, satisfaction, and motivation. It also has a role to play in controlling memory, mood, sleep, learning, concentration, movement, and other bodily functions.

Next there is oxytocin. Oxytocin is your happy hormone; it can literally bring up your mood. Oxytocin can reduce cortisol levels that increase during the stress response, and oxytocin promotes growth and healing.

Lifestyle changes include what you put on your body. Your skin is a giant filter allowing things into your body, and allowing things to leave your body. This means that what you put on your skin goes into the systems in your body. Products that are full of chemicals are getting inside of you and are not moving you toward the healthy end of the path. This is an aspect of health building that is often overlooked.

Also consider what you are breathing in. Air fresheners, chemicals, scented candles, and even off-gassing from furniture and clothes are inhaled into your lungs, which are also a filter into your body. You can't necessarily avoid everything, but some awareness goes a long way. Try switching out air fresheners for essential oil diffusers, scented candles that are full of chemicals for soy candles infused with essential oils, and find personal care products that have natural ingredients rather than lists of chemicals. As I say to my clients, once you learn something, you can't unlearn it. You may just start catching yourself putting that chemical scented product back on the shelf and finding a natural alternative.

Build a Balanced Body

Your body is a very sensitive machine. It needs to be cared for in order for it to function properly. Just because you have cancer or are trying to heal from cancer, doesn't mean your body is broken. It just needs to be rebalanced. How it got out of balance is not important now. What is important is learning to love it where it is, and supporting a healthful and health-building lifestyle.

Thriver Lessons:

✳ Eat whole foods, mostly plants.

✳ Move your body daily.

✳ Lifestyle changes for your body matter.

Episodes from the

"Living to Thrive with Cancer" Podcast

Nutrition and Cancer

Nutrition is important when you have cancer. What you eat during and after cancer matters. It is important to know not just what you should be eating but also how it can be a significant part of your healing process. Simple changes can make a big difference.

Exercise During Cancer

In this guest interview, Coral Levkovitz, fitness instructor and medical student, discusses how exercise while in treatment can support mental health in cancer patients.

Finding Your Energy

Fatigue and a lack of energy are a real problem for people living with cancer. Treatments, surgeries, pain and anxiety can be depleting on the body and energy. It is a kind of tiredness that comes from deep in your core. Learn more about how you can boost your energy through simple actions.

Lifestyle Changes Are Key

Lifestyle changes play a key role in healing from cancer. From changing what you eat to bringing movement and exercise into your life, you can make simple changes can make a big difference.

Creating Your Lifestyle Blueprint

Like a building, your body is all about systems and how they need a strong foundation to build up your body, mind, and spirit. You get to be the architect of your life and the creator of your health.

<u>Yoga for Cancer Support</u>

Yoga holds many benefits for your body, mind, and spirit. Learn more about how yoga can support your life with cancer.

"Your body holds deep wisdom. Trust in it. Learn from it. Nourish it. Watch your life transform and be healthy."

— *Bella Bleue*

Chapter 9

You're Stronger Than You Think

developing the power of your mindset

---

*My oncologist: So I understand you
don't want to know your statistics.
Me: That's right. Every day is a 100% chance
of survival. How is knowing my chances
of living or dying going to serve me?*

One of the first questions I get when I am talking to a new client is, "If you had to do it all again, would you do it the same way?" My answer is always no. I would do all of the learning about food, movement, mindfulness, and spirituality. None of that would change. What I would do differently is not wait to learn about mindset.

At the beginning of my path to thriving, I thought, perhaps like you, that I just needed to change how I ate. I now know that nutrition was the perfect place to start, but I would have also worked on my mindset around how to change how I think and view life, and how to navigate stress and overwhelm.

When I was diagnosed I chose to not get my prognosis because I knew that it didn't feel right for me. I didn't believe that knowing my statistics around the probability of life or death would help me to believe that I could survive. I needed to settle into the belief that every day was a new day and a new opportunity to get up and keep moving forward. This was the first mindset work that I did.

During my first oncology appointment I was given a social worker to talk to. She was lovely, kind, and wanted to help but, she didn't. Two things stand out for me when I think about her. One, I felt like she was preparing me and my family for the most common and perpetuated belief around a stage 4 diagnosis, my inevitable death. The second piece was that her office was at the cancer clinic at the hospital, which required me to walk past all the cancer patients waiting for their appointments. After learning I had cancer, my body now had a visceral reaction to even driving past the cancer clinic, let alone going in it. In order to protect myself, I stopped going.

What I have learned since then is that mindset matters. You can teach your brain how to respond to situations that are triggering and stressful. I now know that having mindfulness practices in my life, which include but are not limited to meditation, is a necessary part of managing stress and calming overwhelm. I have also learned that you can change how you view situations, that you can have language and tools to reduce anxiety, and that you can speak to yourself in a gentle and loving way that runs contrary to the modern fight language that we are used to hearing around cancer. How you talk to yourself matters!

The Stress Response

We cannot talk about cancer without even the word itself bringing up a stress response in the body. This is because your mind is programmed to protect you. Its job is to alert you to danger, and to get you out of the situation. So when there is a perceived danger, your brain activates and deactivates systems in your body to keep you safe, otherwise known as fight or flight.

For cancer patients, the entire process can create triggers around smells, sounds, sights, taste, and touch. As much as you would like to run away, as your brain wants you to, this is a situation where you have to stay and manage it. This can be made a lot easier when you know how to manage your thoughts. Leaving stress unmanaged has an impact on your physical and emotional well-being.

When a situation activates your fight or flight response, you may experience one of more of the following reactions in your body.

* **Physiological reactions**. Heart palpitations, cold sweats, shortness of breath, and headaches are a few examples of how the body responds.

* **Feeling numb.** Your body and your emotions just go still. It is like you can't feel them anymore.

* **Fuzziness in the brain.** It's like trying to look through a foggy window; everything becomes hazy and unclear. Making decisions becomes difficult.

* **Going completely blank**. Your mind, usually buzzing with thoughts, suddenly becomes empty. You know there are thoughts in there but you are not able to access them.

* **Disassociation.** It's as if you're watching the scene unfold from a distance, or to someone else. It's like a movie is happening and you are just standing there watching it.

* **Out-of-body experience.** It is as if you're hovering above yourself, looking down on this surreal moment. Your brain cannot even process that this is happening.

* **The need to run away.** You have an overwhelming urge to escape, and distance yourself from reality. All you want is to feel safe.

All these reactions are totally normal. The problem is that you cannot stay in fight or flight. Inside of your body you are also having a stress hormone response. The stress hormone cortisol is activated and sends the brain into the stress response. When you encounter a stressful situation, your cortisol rises, triggering a chain reaction of physiological responses sending you into fight or flight.

The problem becomes when your cortisol levels are continuously raised. Chronic elevation of cortisol levels can weaken the immune system over time. When you have cancer you need your immune system to be as strong as possible. This is why you need to learn how to navigate and manage stress.

Living with FEAR

Every cancer patient experiences the anxiety around upcoming scans. For some this can start weeks before their scan. It can be especially high the day of the scan and in the following days as you await the results. Your brain is going to tell you all of the stories that will fill you with fear. 'That pain in your side must be cancer.' 'They are going to find a spot.' 'The cancer has come back.' These are real thoughts that can be crippling and can start to control your life if you don't learn how to manage them.

When I talk to my clients about scans and tests we talk about FEAR. I assure them their feeling of fear is normal. This acronym is a tool I use to help them see that as they are experiencing fear it is actually their thoughts that are controlling them and causing them emotional pain.

FEAR stands for *False Evidence Appearing Real*

FEAR is the brain trying to protect you by telling you that something has gone wrong, by giving you this thought so that you will go into fight or flight to protect yourself. The problem is, that this thought raises your cortisol and activates your stress response.

The *false evidence* is that you start to think or even believe that there is a problem. The *appearing real* is that it starts to feel like it is true and that all of the things you fear the most are happening. Your brain is creating thoughts that in turn are creating stories that you tell yourself.

Learning to control the thoughts that lead to FEAR is a powerful tool to have in your toolbox. Unmanaged FEAR keeps you stuck in a belief that something has gone wrong, even when it may not have. Thoughts are powerful. They are stories you tell yourself even when you don't have any supporting evidence. I know you want to get out of FEAR, that you want calm, and that you want to believe that you are alright. I want to offer you a thought that I share with my clients around getting out of FEAR.

Nothing has gone wrong here, until something has gone wrong and if something has gone wrong, then we will deal with it.

What this means is that you very likely don't actually know if something is wrong until you have real proof. In the meantime what you are doing is robbing yourself of today by worrying about a future problem that may not even exist. I know this may feel uncomfortable. If I hadn't done this work on myself, I might be angry at someone for telling me not to have FEAR, but the more you work with this thought, the easier it becomes to prepare yourself for a test, an appointment, or a scan, and the more you will be able to stay present and not project into the unknown future.

Stop Fighting

In the 1970's United States President Richard Nixon declared war on cancer. I believe that since then society has adopted this language around cancer that is based on battle language. People say things like "she fought really hard", "they are kicking cancer's ass", "he is a warrior" and so much more. No doubt you have heard this language being used and perhaps even use it yourself.

For some people this is motivating and inspiring. It provides an image that helps a cancer patient to rally and dig deep. It can inspire them to gather all the resources and get ready for the fight of their life. There is nothing wrong with this; it is not untrue. When you have cancer there is work to be done and I would never tell someone how they should think or feel but I want to offer a different perspective. If someone is vulnerable and afraid, then how can we ask them to fight? Fighting is not synonymous with winning, and winning isn't always the result from fighting.

To give this thought some context think about this: if you had a child or a loved one who was sick and was having a difficult time, would you tell them to get up and keep fighting, to just keep going and to plough ahead, or would you offer them a blanket, a cup of water or tea, a back rub, or a hug? Would you show them softness to help them to feel at ease?

If you bring it back to the stress response, elevated fight language is meant to activate cortisol to prepare the body for a conflict or interaction, but because we now know that stress is not good for the body and that it can compromise the immune system, perhaps it makes sense to you that a softer approach might be what you are looking for. That calm and nurturing language may feel better in your body, mind, and spirit.

I am only offering a perspective that is an option. If this doesn't resonate with you, that is alright. Cancer is an individual experience and you get to manage it in a way that feels right for you.

Becoming Self Aware

Self-awareness is the habit of paying attention to the way you think, feel, and behave. You may or may not even be aware of it, practise it, or think about it. Perhaps it is not in your scope of self-care, or you aren't sure how to introduce it, but it is something that you can learn.

In our busy lives we have a tendency to tune out the messages we receive from our body and our mind. It is human nature to put things off, to wait for another day, and to procrastinate. When it comes to your health, this is not a great course of action.

Self- awareness is not so much the physical as it is the emotional awareness of your thoughts. What we think and how we respond to our thoughts is actually a key part of navigating cancer. Self-awareness allows you to acknowledge what is happening emotionally in your mind and body, and when you can see it for what it is, and really be aware of it, you can then develop tools to navigate those emotions. When you work on your self-awareness it becomes about noticing your patterns of thought. What do you think about and how do you respond to those thoughts? Is it with fear and overwhelm, or with calm and control?

Self-awareness helps you to notice your emotional patterns. You start to see how well you understand your own moods and emotions, you start to observe and try to understand what you are feeling instead of reacting impulsively, and you can stop viewing difficult emotions as problems to be avoided or rid yourself of, and instead see them as messages trying to tell you something.

Finally, self-awareness will help you to see patterns of behaviour. You can start to understand why you tend to act in the same way in certain situations, to notice what types of events are triggering for you, and to understand what motivates your behaviours or leads to self-sabotage. Self-awareness means learning to be curious about your own mind.

Managing Your Mind Matters

Managing your mind is, I think, one of the most powerful tools you can have. Being able to recognize when you are feeling an emotion that is uncomfortable, seeing a thought that comes up that creates stress, and knowing how to bring down your stress is so important. There is so much stress associated with cancer and life after cancer. Positive mindset around emotions sets you up for success. It creates thoughts that help you to understand a situation, and to navigate it.

Learning how to manage your mind begins with a breath. When you breathe in and out you are supporting your body to get out of fight or flight and into rest and reset. Focusing on breath plays a crucial role in supporting relaxation, and is a common technique in mindfulness practices. By paying attention to each inhale and exhale, you bring your awareness to the present moment, which can help reduce focusing on past events or worries about the future, leading to a state of relaxation and peace.

Muscle relaxation and brain support are other responses to deep breathing. By consciously focusing on your breath and taking slow, deep breaths, you can help release tension in the muscles that promotes physical relaxation and increases the supply of oxygen to the brain. Incorporating deep breathing exercises into your daily routine can be an effective way to support relaxation.

Meditation

Many people think that they can't meditate. They think they need to be sitting in a crossed legged position for long periods of time with no thoughts coming up in their mind. This is not true. Meditation can be sitting on a yoga mat, on the grass, walking in the woods, watching the sunset, or whatever else you want it to be. What meditation is, is taking time to slow down and get quiet. It is time to find ease in your body, to feel your emotions, and to breathe.

Grounding

Grounding refers to techniques or practices that help individuals feel more connected, centred, and present in the moment. Grounding can create a great sense of calm and peace, which when you are living with cancer, is very much needed. Different techniques work for different people, so it's essential to explore and find what works best for you. Try standing on the grass barefoot, spending time outdoors, taking a walk in a park, or sitting by a tree. You can even do gentle exercise or even carry or keep objects that have grounding properties for you, such as a smooth stone, a piece of jewellery, or a small item with sentimental value that you can touch or hold onto.

What is important is that you start to recognize when fearful or stressful thoughts are starting to take over and that you bring in tools to manage them. You don't have to live with stress and overwhelm. Knowing how to manage your mind will make a difference in your life with cancer.

Thriver Lessons:

* ✳ FEAR doesn't have to control you.

* ✳ Mindset makes a difference.

* ✳ Your breath is a powerful tool.

Episodes from the

"Living to Thrive with Cancer" Podcast

Mind Your Language

Consider how you talk to yourself. Everything you say integrates into your body, mind, and spirit.

Living with Fear

Understand fear and how you can take back control of your life when you can manage your fear.

Becoming Self Aware

Learn more about how self-awareness is a skill anyone can learn to improve when you have the right tools and a little practice.

Celebrate the Wins

It is important to celebrate the good things that happen in your life. Explore how wins can support your health and happiness.

Mindset Matters

What you think and being able to manage your thoughts is an important part of life with cancer.

Thriving Through Adversity

Sometimes you get news you don't want to hear. It could set you back or you could lean into how to manage it and learn from it.

Power Words

There is a difference between words that emote anger and are a call to fight, and words that empower you to take action and create self-belief. Words make a difference in how you see yourself.

> *Nothing is impossible. The word*
> *itself says "I'm possible."*
>
> *– Audrey Hepburn*

Chapter 10

Believe in Yourself

nurturing self-love and self-belief

My niece: How are you really doing Aunt Kathryn?
Me: I feel like my soul is empty and
I don't know how to fix it.

It was early 2018, three years after my original cancer diagnosis, and I had just had my third cancer related surgery. I was back home trying to put my life back together again. My days were empty because I had quit my job and I felt like I was lost and just existing even though I was living a happy life. I was living in survivor mode.

I knew I couldn't keep feeling this way, but I also didn't know what I was feeling. It was like there was a grey filter over my life, like the kind you add to a picture only not the bright cheery type. It dimmed everything leaving me feeling empty, and like something was missing. I knew there had to be more to life after cancer than this. I wanted to feel whole again and stop feeling stuck.

My niece came over for tea one day and as we sat in the living room talking, she asked me how I was doing. I told her I felt like something was missing, that my soul felt empty. She suggested that I take yoga teacher training. I told her I wasn't interested in becoming a yoga teacher, but she insisted that this may be just the way to help me reconnect with myself. Having nothing to lose, I signed up. It was the best and most timely decision I could have made. Just a few months into training they found a metastasis in my right lung. The weekend before graduation from my training program I had my fourth cancer related surgery.

This time was different from previous surgeries. This time I had tools to help me manage – a stronger body, strong self-belief, a community to lift me up, and the power of my breath. I went into this surgery strong, confident, and calmer than ever before.

This was the start of my realisation that the tools that I had learned in yoga would forever be part of my healing process. That was when I knew that I needed to explore other holistic modalities and gather more tools that would create healing in my body, mind, and spirit, which, I believe is what we are all looking for. Yoga taught me to breathe when I was overwhelmed, to love myself for who I am, to love my body for what it has experienced, and to find peace through mindfulness practices and to be grateful every single day.

From Surviving to Thriving with Cancer

When I look back to where I was before I gathered all these tools, I really was in survivor mode. I didn't know who I was or where I wanted to go. My soul was empty. Now I could see that I was capable of moving from just surviving, into thriving in my life. No longer were external circumstances controlling my life where it felt like things were happening to me. This was the beginning of the internal growth that led me to want to not just support myself, but support other people living with cancer. This was the first step into becoming a Holistic Cancer Coach and into a life of wholly and completely thriving.

You Can't Stay Stuck

People, like me in my story above, often feel stuck when they are diagnosed with cancer. There are a lot of reasons during your walk with cancer where these reasons can come up. The first time you feel stuck may be right after the doctor has told you that you have cancer. The stress response and how your brain reacts to traumatising news can create a feeling of being stuck in your physical body, in your emotional responses, or in your inability to think and respond. Another time you may feel stuck may be when you want to get support and start taking care of yourself, but you are overwhelmed by information, choices, lack of information, misinformation and more. Perhaps you are stuck in making decisions and having clarity. Or, perhaps you are now in the post cancer part of your life and are trying to get your life back on track but the side effects of treatment, and the impact physically and emotionally on your body feels like a challenge. These and other situations can cause you to feel like you can't make decisions, can't move forward, and are just stuck in one place.

Loss of control is another real aspect of cancer that causes you to feel stuck. Cancer can make you feel like you've lost control over your body and life. Treatment plans, side effects, and changes in lifestyle disrupt your sense of control and normalcy. I want you to know that you actually have a lot more control that you may think you have. You can control what you eat, what cleaning products you use, how much exercise you get, what type of exercise you do, when you see people and when you don't, and so much more.

This feeling of being stuck can physically and emotionally drain you. This is the perfect time to bring in mindfulness practices to help you to feel like you are taking steps to support yourself. This is also when you need to call in help. You don't have to do this alone.

This is where you access your superpower of asking for help. Who you ask, and what you ask for can be in your control, which can help you to start moving forward in life.

Love Yourself

Self-love is the practice of caring for, accepting, and valuing yourself. It is you treating yourself with kindness, compassion, and respect. Self-love includes both a deep appreciation for your strengths and acknowledgment of your weaknesses without being hard on yourself. Inside of each of us is a version of ourself that is our own worst critic, the version that puts everyone else first, and the version that questions and doubts ourself. This can create self-limiting thoughts that will hold you back from stepping out of survivor mode and into thriver mode.

Loving yourself is important because you matter. The idea of loving yourself can feel really challenging. This can be especially overwhelming when your body has changed, your memory is compromised, and your anxiety is through the roof. When you practise self-love, you cultivate positive emotions such as happiness, contentment, and inner peace. This can lead to improved mental health and resilience in the face of challenges. By treating yourself with kindness, you boost your self-confidence and self-esteem. This can empower you to manage your fears, try new strategies and tools to support yourself, and assert yourself in ways you may not have before cancer. When you love yourself, you can start to see what you need and to take action to get it. This is not selfish. This is self-love.

Another way to think about it is the idea that you are a name on a list of people that are important in your life. I had a client tell me once that often she was at the bottom of the list, and that usually she wasn't even on the list. This is the list of self-care, the list of what gets prioritised in your life. We have been socialised to put other people first. This is good in theory, but not so good if you have cancer.

When you have cancer, you need to move yourself up to the top of the list, not at the expense of others, but in the best interest of yourself. Every ounce of you and your energy is needed to support your body, mind, and spirit. Engaging in self-care practices such as exercise, proper nutrition, and adequate sleep are all manifestations of self-love, leading to improved overall health and well-being. The goal is to do everything you can to take back your life and your health. You need to be at the top of your list.

Self-love also helps to support you when things feel challenging. When you have a strong sense of self-love, you're better equipped to cope with setbacks, criticism, and failures. Instead of viewing setbacks as flaws, you're more likely to view them as opportunities for growth, and when you love yourself, you're more likely to pursue activities and goals that align with your values and passions, leading to a greater sense of fulfilment in life. This is all part of learning and growing from cancer. In essence, self-love is the foundation for a fulfilling and meaningful life, even when you have cancer. By cultivating a compassionate and accepting relationship with yourself, you can navigate the challenges with greater resilience, foster healthier connections with others, and ultimately, live a more joyful and purposeful life right now.

Self-Belief is Key

Believing in yourself when facing cancer is so important and, I think, is one of the most important pieces of work you can do when you have been given a diagnosis.

This is part of the reason I am not a fan of cancer statistics being delivered in a way that takes away hope, because it also takes away self-belief. Believing that you can do this is a critical piece of moving through your cancer process. Self-belief empowers you to take an active role in your treatment decisions and overall well-being. It allows you to advocate for yourself, ask questions, and participate in your care plan more effectively. Believing in yourself can provide the mental strength needed for the challenges of everyday life and for maintaining a positive outlook. When you believe in yourself, you are telling your brain that fear and overwhelming thoughts aren't going to control you, and that you are taking back control over your life, focusing on what you can do rather than what you can't.

Finally, self-belief can help you to maintain a positive mindset which can improve your overall quality of life and even positively impact your treatment outcomes. Believing in yourself activates your happy hormones and can give you the lift you need to help you stay optimistic. This lift helps to lower your stress, which can boost your immune system, which in turn will support your health. Your body is amazing. It doesn't operate in isolation. Instead it works together to support you. When you believe in yourself you are sending the message to your body that you are there for it and that you will help it to get better.

Self-love and self-belief are the inner work that gives you not only physical tools to support yourself, but connects you with your spirit, and your essence of who you are. That piece will not only keep you present in the now, it will also help you to move yourself forward into a thriving life.

Mantra and Positive Affirmations

One of my favourite tools for bringing myself back when my brain and emotions take over, is mantra and positive affirmations. This has been an important part of my own healing. I believe wholly and completely that if we can talk ourselves into negative thoughts and beliefs, then we can also talk ourselves into positive self-love and self-belief. Mantra, is a form of meditation that involves repeating a sacred sound, word, or phrase that helps to focus the mind and support relaxation. It is a way to bring yourself back inside to stop negative thoughts and fears from getting away from you. By giving your mind a simple task to focus on, you support your mind in allowing your thoughts and worries to fade away. Mantra also helps you to create self-love and self-belief, which are key factors in learning how to live with cancer.

Mantras and affirmations are very personal. Find ones that resonate with you personally. You can even create your own statement based on what you believe and want. Just remember that the intention is to release negative thoughts and feelings and replace them with self-love and self-belief because they can serve as powerful tools for maintaining a positive mindset and promoting emotional well-being throughout your healing.

Mantras and positive affirmations
for comfort and strength

*"I am surrounded by love and support, and
I draw strength from those around me."*

*"With each breath, I fill myself with healing
energy and release any negativity."*

"My body is strong, resilient, and capable of healing."

*"I trust in the wisdom of my body
to heal and restore itself."*

"I am happy, I am healthy."

*"I am not defined by my illness; I am
defined by my strength and resilience."*

*"Every day, in every way, I am getting
stronger and healthier."*

*"I embrace each moment with gratitude
and positivity, knowing that every step
forward is a beautiful gift."*

*"I am guided by hope and faith, knowing
that brighter days lie ahead."*

*"I am worthy of love, joy, and good health,
and I actively invite these into my life."*

*"I am facing my challenges with courage,
grace and determination".*

and my favourite…

"I am a beautiful miracle."

The Power of Rest

Rest is often an unsung hero in the cancer process. It is also often resisted because it can be seen as weakness. In our society we are taught to push on, keep moving forward, not stop and get things done. Rest is crucial for your body to heal.

The body undergoes immense stress during cancer treatment. Rest allows the body to redirect energy towards healing and recovery. Your cells need time to heal and that time is when your body is sending all of your energy to the cells. Adequate rest is also essential for maintaining a strong immune system. Cancer treatments can weaken the immune system, making patients more susceptible to infections. Rest helps the body conserve energy and resources to bolster immune function which is so important.

Cancer and its treatments often create extreme fatigue. Rest helps alleviate this fatigue, improving overall quality of life and allowing patients to better cope with their treatment regimens. As well, cancer treatments frequently come with various side effects. Rest can alleviate some of these symptoms and provide relief from treatment-related distress.

Coping with cancer can be emotionally draining. Rest provides an opportunity for you to relax, reduce stress, and engage in activities that promote mental well-being, such as meditation, mindfulness, or simply spending time with loved ones.

Heed the need for rest as part of nurturing self-love and self-belief. Rest plays a critical role in your care, supporting both physical and emotional well-being throughout your healing process.

Having a Purpose

The final piece in nurturing self-love and self-belief is having a purpose. Needing a purpose while facing cancer is a deeply personal matter, and you may approach it differently based on your beliefs, values, and coping mechanisms than someone else reading this book. My purpose from the beginning was my family, as I am sure it is for so many of you. As I moved through the years, grateful to be a thriver, I felt compelled to do something with the gift of my life. I knew I wanted to do more but I wasn't sure what it was. I had been a teacher. I loved teaching and supporting others and I loved creating content and lessons, but I honestly didn't think that there was any other job for me that would allow me to use these skills, until I discovered coaching.

Before cancer I wasn't really aware of the idea of life coaches, as they are relatively new to the wellness world, but as I started to look around, and even hired my own coach to support me, I saw a hole and I knew that was what I needed to do. I needed to fill that hole by becoming a Certified Holistic Cancer Coach. The holistic part was really important to me because I was learning that cancer isn't all about the medicine and the medical process. Cancer is a very human experience in real people with real needs. Cancer patients can use conventional medicine, but they can also use holistic tools, like we are talking about in this book, to support their body, mind, and spirit. In fact, I wish that I had a coach when I was going through the initial cancer process of appointments, surgeries and treatments. I remember having so many thoughts and emotions that I didn't know how to navigate or even understand. I would have loved guidance on how to bring in holistic modalities to ease my pain, manage my thoughts, and support my spirit.

Having a purpose has made a huge difference in my life of living with cancer. Purpose can provide a sense of meaning and direction, which can be particularly important when things feel challenging. Purpose can help you to focus on something beyond your illness and find significance in your experience. I see so many cancer survivors raising money, sharing their stories to support others, participating in cancer walks and runs, and so much more. A purpose can serve as a source of motivation to keep moving forward, whether it's for yourself, your loved ones, or a cause. It can provide the strength needed to navigate difficult treatments and maintain self-love and self-belief. It can contribute to an improved quality of life by fostering a sense of fulfilment, satisfaction, and connection with others. It can help counteract feelings of helplessness and despair.

I remember when I was in the hospital for my first surgery, my right hemicolectomy, there was a whiteboard at the foot of my bed. At the bottom of it, it said, "My Goal is…" I joke now that probably it was meant to encourage the patient to set a goal of getting up and going for a walk, or eating solid food or something big and health related.

I saw this prompt and turned to my husband and said, *"I am going to run another marathon."* And we did. We trained for it, we called in our marathon running friends, and they flew in from across the country to run the Scotiabank Waterfront Marathon 2017 with me. That decision became a purpose, to prove to myself that not only would I survive cancer, but that I would run another marathon to show cancer that I was in control and that I was a thriver. Having a purpose cultivates resilience, enabling you to overcome adversity and to bounce back from setbacks. It provides a reason to keep moving forward despite the obstacles you face. It provides hope. Let me leave you with this mantra around purpose:

"Not today cancer, I have things to do.

Thriver Lessons:

* Getting unstuck can change your life.

* Self-love and self-belief are key to healing.

* Find your purpose and feel empowered.

Episodes from the

"Living to Thrive with Cancer" Podcast

The Power of Rest

Health and healing happens best when your body is calm and rest is part of that. Learn more about the power of rest in your life.

Courageous Choices

Explore the profound courage it takes to navigate life with cancer. Uncover the power of bravery and how it shapes our path to thriving.

Learning and Growing From Cancer

Discover how facing this challenge is an opportunity for meaningful change, leading to a new perspective on living with cancer.

You Can Be Exceptional

This is a reminder of all the opportunities that are available to you to support your health and healing and to help you be exceptional.

Service and Purpose

Discover the power of purpose in moving beyond survival. Find motivation, personal value, and fulfilment in daily life with purpose.

The Simple Way to Find Calm and Rest

Discover the simplicity of finding calm and rest with nature's support. Explore how nature enhances relaxation in your daily life effortlessly.

Thriving is a Body, Mind, and Spirit Journey

There is a way to move forward that includes supporting your body, mind, and spirit. Learn more about a holistic approach to moving from survivor to thriver.

Living with Cancer

Dive into how reframing a diagnosis makes it possible to look at a cancer diagnosis in a different way.

> *"I love when people that have been through hell walk out of the flames carrying buckets of water for those still consumed by the fire."*
> — *Stephanie Sparkles*

Chapter 11

Living to Thrive

from survivor to thriver

My doctor: I'd like to share a concept with you –
it's called living with cancer. I think it will help.

In November 2017, I received two very different phone calls. The first was from my oncologist to tell me that they had found another cancerous mass in my abdomen. This phone call took me back to the first time they told me I had cancer. I was angry, distressed, overwhelmed, afraid… everything I had felt the first time around except this time there was another layer added. Reoccurrence. I had only been No Evidence of Disease, otherwise known as "cancer free", for less than two years and here I was again facing uncertainty and fear.

The second phone call came from my doctor who had managed my chemotherapy at my local hospital. When I answered the phone, I wasn't sure what to expect. What more could there possibly be? The voice on the other end of the line said, "I wanted to call to tell you how sorry I am that this is happening to you again." She went on to ask if I was open to having a conversation about the future. What she shared with me in that brief call has changed my life and my perspective on having cancer forever. She said, "I'd like to share a concept with you – it's called living with cancer. I think it will help." And it has.

Since that phone call I have had more reoccurrences. Each has become easier to manage because of one thought – living with cancer is possible. It needs to be said that possible and easy are not the same thing. Cancer is by no means easy as you know. It is daily work to navigate what to eat, how to take care of yourself, all the emotions, the fears, the sneaky thoughts, the whispers in your mind, and the changes in your relationship with yourself and others. There is the ongoing vigilance required in the monitoring of your body while you are trying to live your life. Because I have learned how to live with cancer, I have learned that this is more manageable.

Learning to Live with Cancer

When my doctor first used the term living with cancer, I will admit I prickled. I was offended. I was angry. The idea of living with cancer implies that I will never be cured and I will just have to deal with it. What got my attention was when my doctor said she thought the concept would help. I unclenched my jaw and tried to be open to listening. That is when everything changed.

She shared with me that living with cancer is about the patient taking control of their life. It is about getting off the cancer roller coaster where you are living an almost manic existence of joy and relief one moment, and grief and anger the next. It is a concept meant to help you level the playing field rather than living in highs and lows.

To best understand what living with cancer means, my doctor shared this analogy: consider someone with a chronic illness. They are living with a condition that requires ongoing attention. They may need to take injections every day, develop pain management strategies, do regular medical procedures, or take medications to support their health. They need to know what to do when things feel off, which requires them to have a high level of self-awareness when it comes to their body. In addition to this, they require ongoing medical support to keep them moving forward and to ensure changes in their health are addressed. They have a support team to optimise their health and in turn their life. This fosters the creation of life supporting habits, beginning as what 'must be done,' and at a certain point it becomes a way of living rather than a day-to-day struggle and effort. It is the same with cancer.

Cancer is a chronic illness that can be managed. It requires vigilance and monitoring in your body. You can make choices that keep you on the roller coaster living in fear and stress, or you can decide to get off the scary ride, and feel more level and in control day to day. When you shift your mindset to a place of acceptance, the day to day becomes more manageable.

Living with cancer is about the life you are living right now. It is about staying out of fear of the future, and instead living in the present to enjoy life right now. Embracing that you are living with cancer means you are deciding to do what you can when you can.

You Have a Lot to Figure Out

Cancer survivors have a lot to figure out and I would be lying if I said this was easy. Remember, possible and easy are not the same thing. This is where self-belief is important. My clients share with me the grief they feel around loss of control and how their lives have changed.

Believing in yourself will help you bring into your life the concepts that I have shared in this book and will put you on the path to thriving. You don't have to control everything. You only need to control what you can and what matters to you.

The concept of struggle is ingrained in us as humans. Success does not have to be a struggle. Stop using the negative fight language of a victim and instead figure out how to claim your power that will move you into thriving. This is the essence of living to thrive – creating your version of life with cancer that allows you to live your life each day, follow what you are called to do, and learn how to move through surviving to thriving.

Empowerment Through Impediments

There are going to be moments throughout your life with cancer when you feel like a wall has been thrown up in front of you. There will be choices to be made and emotions to be navigated to move forward. Consider a hurdle versus an obstacle. A "hurdle" will slow you down as you move forward, but an "obstacle" will stop you where you are. You can choose whether something is a hurdle or an obstacle. Then you can make the choice of how you are going to move forward.

* **Returning to work**. Some of you will choose to return to work in order to get back to normal, while others may financially have no other choice. Some of you may not return to the workplace at all because of the physical and emotional changes you have experienced. Ultimately, this is a very personal decision.

* **Changes to your body.** Healing is a process. Those of you who have had physically altering surgeries need to learn how to love your body as it is now. It will require a tremendous amount of self-compassion. Your scars are very personal – they are a sign of victory and personal triumph. Don't allow your scars to stop you from living. Get support if you are struggling so that you can feel whole again.

* **Fear.** Do not permit fear, stress, and anxiety to run your life. You need to emotionally and

mentally process what you are experiencing. Consciously choose to recognize, identify, and manage overwhelming thoughts and fears. Avoiding them will not help you move forward. Knowing how to manage your thoughts and feelings will make a difference in your life and will give you courage.

* **Feeling Stuck.** Your experience of feeling stuck will prevent you from moving forward. Find a sense of empowerment so you can be present in all that you do. Learn more about yourself and your needs. This will enable you to take the necessary steps to move forward.

* **Socially you may not feel the same.** Getting together with friends or going out can be difficult. Try to remember that your friends and family love you. You will have to decide how or if you respond to peoples' comments and questions. You will have to decide whether to go out at all. You may even have to come to terms with the fact that some of your old friends are no longer part of your life. Allow yourself the freedom to choose what feels best for you and how you want to live your life.

✳ **Triggers will happen.** Triggers are reminders of past incidents – sights, sounds, smells, and situations can all bring up an intense stress response. So much of living with cancer comes back to learning how to manage your mind. Use your tools and strategies to support yourself when you feel a response to a trigger. Pause and sit with the thought or feeling you are having. Meditate. Breathe. Bring yourself back to the present. Remind yourself that this is a physical and emotional response to a past event. That was then. It is not right now. The past can have a grip on your life if you stay stuck in it. Do not let negative thoughts about the past project to the future and leave you feeling powerless in the present.

I want to offer you this - allow yourself to rebuild your life with ease and grace. You have been through a lot; it is going to take time to trust your body and yourself, and to believe that you are okay. You may have to give yourself permission to move at your own pace, to say yes when it feels right, and no when it doesn't. This is where the body, mind, and spirit work come in and where you create your holistic healing process. Here is where self-love, self-care, and self-belief matter.

Be Triumphant

One of my favourite moments on a call with a client is when they share a win. It doesn't matter whether it is a big event like clear scans or something smaller like going for a walk– a win is a win and we celebrate them all.

As you move forward on this path to thriving you will have moments that will stand out for you as a benchmark of how far you have come – physically, emotionally, and spiritually. Own all of them. They matter. In a world where it can feel heavy and like there is so much going against you, you need to see and feel when the good stuff happens.

* **Find Yourself.** One of the greatest gifts I have discovered in my life with cancer is myself. Because I have spent a lot of time in my thoughts – good and bad – I have had time to see who I was and who I want to be now. You may experience something similar. There are so many lessons that come out of this that can foster the opportunity to learn who you really are and to develop self-love. You may notice yourself having different interests than you used to, or wanting to take your life in a different

direction. Loving yourself is important because you matter. It is the opportunity to connect to your spirit.

* **Reinvent yourself.** Out of change comes the opportunity to reinvent yourself. So many of my clients talk about wanting to do something with their cancer story to make changes not just in their life but in the lives of others. Some find the work they were doing previously feels empty or meaningless since experiencing this life changing event. Instead, they want to live a purposeful life and feel fulfilled. You can reinvent yourself. It may not come quickly but it will happen.

* **Seek clarity.** This is a big one. Cancer has changed my life – for the better. Ironically, I am the happiest and healthiest that I have ever been. I LOVE this new version of me. I am kinder, happier, and loving life more than I ever have. Clarity is everything; don't waste your life on what is not important. Possessions don't matter. Outside noise from the media shouldn't take up your mental space. Do not spend time with disingenuous people. Let's be honest - when you have faced cancer and the threat of dying, there

are a lot of things that used to seem like a big deal that no longer are. Living your life to the fullest right now is what is important. You get to decide who and what you want to spend your time and energy on. Live your life out loud! Have fun, laugh, dance, paint, sing out loud, do what fills your heart with joy, and embrace every opportunity you have to be alive.

* **Inner strength.** There are often no words to describe how you manage to get up every day and keep moving forward when your thoughts are trying to hold you back. It takes a lot of courage to come to terms with the fact that you have cancer, to decide that you are going to take control of your life, and dig deep every day to keep moving forward. In the face of adversity, the human spirit can do amazing things. You are stronger than you think and you can do this.

* **Be confident.** Change your mindset and find your voice to become more confident in your thoughts and decisions. Cancer has forced you to make choices while you are the most vulnerable you have ever been. There is a lot of empowerment in this. Every choice you make

is creating a thriving version of yourself. You get to decide.

Your Relationship with Cancer

Throughout this book I have shared with you pieces of my story that have been important in how I have learned to see myself and cancer. I have created a relationship with cancer and you have too. You do not own it. It is not who you are. Do not allow it to define how you live your life. Choose not to refer to it as *my* cancer but instead as *the* cancer.

We have a little dance, the cancer and I – we do the required tests and scans, we wait for the results, we make big and little decisions based on what the cancer has brought into my life, and we stare each other in the eye from time to time. Some days it feels like it is trying to take back control. Other days I feel like I have total control. Sometimes it isn't even a thought.

If I had not adopted the doctor's concept of living with cancer, I truly do not think my life would be this way. For the first three years, cancer held the reins and guided me down the path I am walking. But, with one phone call and the willingness to have an open mind, I took control. I am completely aware that cancer will always be part of my life – how can it not be? It has reshaped me literally and figuratively and it has changed my relationship with myself and that of my family. It has closed doors that have allowed me to open new ones and it has given me the belief in myself that I need as I live with cancer. It can do this for you too.

You Can

If you take anything from this book, my hope is that you believe that you can do this. When you move past self-limiting thoughts and those imposed by society's script of what life with cancer looks like, there is a whole other way of living available to you in which you can thrive.

I invite you to go to the mirror and read these statements out loud to yourself with confidence.

✳ I can learn how to live with cancer.

✳ I am not my diagnosis.

✳ I can get off the roller coaster and find calm.

✳ I am beautiful inside and out.

✳ I can ask for help.

✳ I can love and nurture my body.

✳ I can reclaim my life and transform my health.

✳ I can do the work to get and stay healthy in a way that feels good for me.

✳ I can navigate the ups and downs of how I am feeling.

✳ I am empowered when I use tools and strategies.

* I can decide what I want to do and how I want to live.

* I am in control of my thoughts and my life.

* I love myself.

* I am strong.

* I believe in myself.

* I can move beyond just surviving day to day.

* I am here.

* I can live my life to my fullest, follow my heart and thrive in all I do.

This is living to thrive with cancer.

My name is Kathryn and I am a cancer THRIVER.

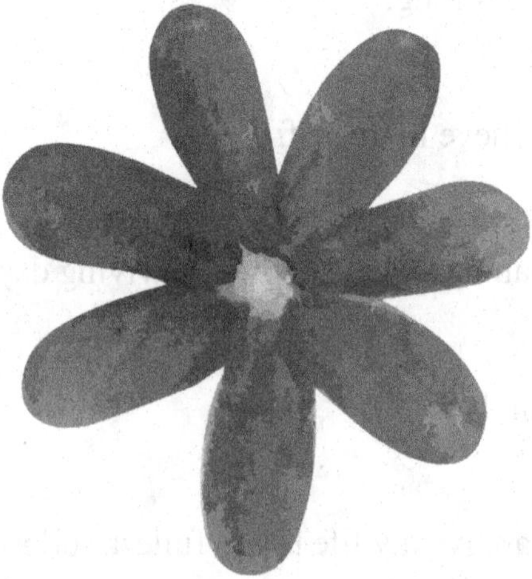

Acknowledgments

In my life with cancer I have learned that gratitude is an important part of healing. This book is part of my healing and would not have happened without the love, encouragement, and support of so many.

I am forever grateful to my husband and sons who have walked with me from the beginning.

To my husband, Jonathan White, I love you more than I can put into words. You are a giver. You made the hardest days possible with your unconditional love and support. I don't know that I could have done this without you at my side.

To my sons Jackson White and Joshua White – your support, belief in me, openness to all of my ideas, and your love have carried me through. I know this has been difficult for both of you. I am grateful you have each other.

Thank you to my beautiful family for supporting me in the writing of this book. I know that this life with cancer has impacted you as much as it has impacted me. I believe in my heart that it has helped each of us to grow and heal. You are my reason to live.

To all of the medical practitioners for their care that set me on the path to healing so that I could pick up the torch to take it further and deeper. To my sister-in-law Laurie Annaert, who was one of the first people in my medical care team and who supported us as we navigated the medical world. To Dr. Hugh McLachlin, the surgeon who listened to me and found the cancer. You saved my life. There are no words to truly express the thanks and the gratitude I feel. To my oncologist, Dr. Stephen Welch for your compassion and belief in me from the first time we met. You have walked this walk with me for the past nine years, always being honest and open. Your care is the bar that I hope all oncologists will rise to. To Dr. Paula Donahue who introduced me to the concept of Living with Cancer, a concept that changed how I viewed cancer and allowed me to learn how to live.

To my own coaches Kelli Youngman, Amanda Grace, and Emma O'Connor who taught me how to see myself for who I am, to love myself again, and to believe in myself so that I could be happy and healthy.

To my husband Jonathan, my friends Marla Morrison and Jackie Scott, and our loving cousins Michael and Cathy Bachner, who walked through this book with me providing me with insights, suggestions, and emotional support along the way.

To Carl Wagner from the Center for the Advancement in Cancer Education and BeatCancer. org for your work in holistic cancer care education, and for writing the forward to my first book. The Holistic Cancer Coach Certification that I received from your Center has allowed me to grow personally and to serve others who are seeking a different way to move through their cancer diagnosis.

And, finally to everyone who has followed me and supported me from my diagnosis, through all of the surgeries and the treatments. To the women who came to my nutrition classes in my early days of wanting to help others to learn how to be healthy. To my yoga teachers and yoga students who helped me to learn more about healing through the body, mind, and spirit. To all of the beautiful souls I have met along the path who have entrusted me with their most sacred possession – their self. You inspire me every day.

About the Author

Kathryn White, CD, BA, BEd, E-RYT200, HCC is an author, presenter, podcaster, and holistic cancer coach.

Kathryn was an elementary school teacher for almost twenty years until 2015, when she was diagnosed with Stage 4 Colon Cancer. This led to her leave teaching permanently to regain her health. After recovering from treatment, Kathryn was determined to rediscover herself and what she wanted from her new lease on life. She set out to learn more about how to prevent colon cancer and how to live healthy.

Never far from her original calling as a teacher, Kathryn successfully completed a certification as a Culinary Nutrition Expert, which led her to launch her own business running workshops and providing personalised nutrition planning for people wanting to change their own lives and prevent disease. The next step in her personal road to health and healing was to become an E-RYT 200 hour registered yoga teacher with a focus on trauma informed yoga, yin and restorative yoga, meditation, and mindfulness.

As a continuation of her desire to educate others about healthy lifestyles and cancer prevention, Kathryn earned her certification as a Holistic Cancer Coach in 2021. Since then she has gone on to support numerous other women through personalised cancer coaching and group programs. She supports women living with a cancer diagnosis to reclaim their life, transform their health, and move beyond just surviving to start thriving in their life.

To share her message of self-belief and possibility, Kathryn created and hosts the *"Living to Thrive with Cancer"* Podcast. She has participated as a panelist at the Colorectal Cancer Canada Annual Virtual Conference, been a guest speaker at the Colorectal Cancer Canada Women's All About You Event, the Toronto Yoga Show, and the She is Me Virtual Conference. Kathryn has been featured on numerous podcasts and online talks. She is a strong advocate for cancer prevention and integrating holistic modalities into cancer healing.

Kathryn has authored numerous articles, and hosts a blog for people wanting support and strategies for living with cancer. She maintains a private virtual coaching practice, where her clients benefit from her personal lived experience with cancer as they navigate their own walk with cancer. She is the proud owner of Kathryn White Wellness.

In her off time, Kathryn enjoys reading, hiking, camping, travelling, and spending time with her husband Jonathan and her two adult sons, Jackson and Joshua.

Let's Stay Connected

Kathryn White Wellness

hello@kathrynwhite.coach

Printed in the United States
by Baker & Taylor Publisher Services